S.Y.N.C.

Self-Employment, Your New Career

Avoid costly mistakes by taking the steps inside!!!

This book is not geared toward a specific industry or time.

It is for every small business and some individuals.

By

Mamie A. Brinkley

Self-Employment, Your New Career

Avoid costly mistakes by taking the proper steps

Published in Nashville, Tennessee by MJBF Publishing Company

ISBN #   13: 978-0615962146   (MJBF Publishing Company)
ISBN #   10: 0615962149

Printed in the United States of America

This publication may be purchased in bulk for educational or business use.

For information please email

mab@mamiebrinkley.com

Dedication

I am thankful for my Lord and Savior in directing his angels to watch over me constantly and assure me that I am being protected and taken care of at all times from harm.

I am most thankful to my dad and mom, Milton J. Brinkley and Marietta A. Brinkley, for bringing me into existence and instilling in me a great educational foundation from which to grow. I thank them for teaching me to be self-sufficient and accepting every day as a new adventure. I thank my dad for always having an answer for any question I could come up with and my mom for always going after the dream.

I am also thankful for my son, Mershard J. B. Frierson, who without him coming along I am sure my life would not have been nearly as exciting or invigorating as it has been since his presence. I am blessed to have had a child who has "all that and a bag of chips".

Mamie A. Brinkley

Step by step process of how to start, run and maintain your business

Table of Contents

Reference Materials and Checklists
Located in Back of this Publication

Welcome

Have you ever considered the question of "Do I have a passion for what I do every day to earn a living?   Or "Am I happy with my present financial status?"

If your answer to either question was a resounding NO, then you may be one of the 70% to 85% of Americans that probably should be self-employed.

This publication is here to assist you with your decision to become happy with your daily work performance and hopefully increase your financial stability at the same time.

I encourage you to just get started, on a certain and distinct path. Enjoy the journey, but do not quit your day job just yet. Think of where you are now as the beginning of the bridge you are about to cross and now is the time to pack your bags and prepare yourself and family for this awesome journey beckoning you.

We are excited for you to begin your journey and will be available for assistance should questions or concerns arise.

Mamie Brinkley

Introduction

Rules for Success

BECOME SELF-SUFFICIENT, SELF-RELIANT AND SELF-EMPLOYED

Keep an open mind and
learn to dispel common business myths.

CHALLENGES

A challenge is an invitation to try something
new and expand your horizons

Introduction

We appreciate the consideration you are giving to our publication to assist you in your mission of the wonderful adventure of becoming self-sufficient, self-reliant and, of course, self-employed.

Your decision is one of the largest considerations you will make in your career and hopefully one of the most fruitful and rewarding. More importantly, obtaining accurate information and being confident in your trade of interest and passion plays a major role in your success.

Many people work for most of their lives in fields and industries just to make a living and never realize their dreams of doing the work which they have a passion. Only about five to twenty percent (5% to 20%) of all people do what they love doing, and then just so happen to make a living. Some people make lots of money, others sometime continue to struggle, but they do not dream their dream.

Many of us have wondered about the world of "Self-Employment". We have delved into various hobbies, business ventures and multi-level marketing groups. In addition to these ventures you continue working for a regular paycheck with little regard for our own happiness. We spend the majority of our workday doing something we probably don't like, just to collect a pay check at the end.

Where is the passion for what you do when earning money?

The passion could range from several things such as carpentry cooking, driving, sewing, and playing with dirt to creating something unique.

This book will assist the new aspiring entrepreneur to take the next big step into their own enterprise. It will also help the seasoned business owner who may not have reviewed certain aspects of their business on this level in the past. It will also bring to the forefront certain processing methods which could possibly reduce your income tax bill by capturing all transactions which may be tax deductible.

Although most self employment books and reference materials begin with a business plan, we will begin on a simpler note.

This book will put aside many myths and hearsays about the "how to do" business and help you to make your venture a successful one.

In a many cases, people do not do what their initial inclination tells them to do because it may seem to be such a long shot. When you have these perceptions you may have, in the past, had a tendency to be docile because of fear and therefore, not being as productive of at pursuing your passion as you should have been.

This publication will assist you in taking those positive, aggressive and fruitful steps toward putting your intentions and passions into place. It will help you to have a fluid transition from being dependent upon someone else for your career path, to taking control of your own destiny and making the investment in yourself to excel in your own enhancements and business journey.

"Risk is the price you pay for the possibility of opportunity"

I believe that all people, at some point in their life, need to travel abroad. While traveling abroad, I found many unique business experiences. In Mexico it was "Chit lets". In Thailand it was "Pokémon Cards". Our system of conducting business and tax platform in America excels many other countries, however, we, as Americans do not always push ourselves to our top potential.

Take a chance, expect the best
and see things in a different way.

The Entrepreneur's Quiz

Let's take a few minutes to go through a whimsical quiz just to get started.

The Entrepreneur's Quiz is the result of a collective investigation of individuals who are presently self-employed. Although the quiz lacks the supportive statistical backup, I offer it as an insight into the entrepreneurial philosophy. Why not try it yourself to see if you've got what it takes to be an entrepreneur? You can even score it in the privacy of your home or office. No one needs to know the real truth about you if you decide not to share.

1. An entrepreneur is most commonly the _____ child in the family.

       a.   oldest
       b.   middle
       c.   youngest
       d.   doesn't matter

2. An entrepreneur is most commonly:

       a.   married
       b.   single
       c.   widowed
       d.   divorced

3. An entrepreneur is most typically a

       a.   man
       b.   woman
       c.   either

4. An individual usually begins his first entrepreneurial company at which age?

       a .   teens
       b.   twenties
       c.   thirties
       d   forties
       e.   fifties

S.Y.N.C.

5. Usually an individual's entrepreneurial tendency first appears evident at which of these stages?

      a.   teens
      b.   twenties
      c.   thirties
      d.   forties
      e.   fifties

6. Typically, an entrepreneur has achieved the following educational attainment by the time he begins his first serious business venture:

      a.   grammar school
      b.   high school diploma
      c.   bachelor's degree
      d.   master's degree
      e.   Doctoral degree

7. An entrepreneur's primary motivation for starting his own business is:

      a.   to make money
      b.   because they can't work for anyone else
      c.   to be famous
      d.   as an outlet for unused energy

8. The primary motivation for the entrepreneur's high ego and need for achievement is based upon his relationship with:

      a.   his wife
      b.   his brother
      c.   his father
      d.   his children

9. An entrepreneur brings which of these items from business to business:

      a.   desk
      b.   chair
      c.   all office furniture
      d.   none of these items

10. To be successful in an entrepreneurial venture you need an over abundance of:

      a.   money
      b.   luck/blessings
      c.   hard work
      d.   good ideas

S.Y.N.C.

11. Entrepreneurs and venture capitalists:

      a.   gets along well
      b.   are the best of friends
      c.   are cordial friends
      d.   are in secret conflict

12. A successful entrepreneur relies on which of these groups for critical management advice:

      a.   internal management team
      b.   external management professionals
      c.   financial sources
      d.   no one

13. Entrepreneurs are best as:

      a.   managers
      b.   venture capitalists
      c.   planners
      d.   doers

14. Entrepreneurs are:

      a.   high risk takers (big gamblers)
      b.   moderate risk takers (realistic gamblers)
      c.   small risk takers (take few chances)
      d.   doesn't matter

15. The only necessary and sufficient ingredient for starting a business is:

      a.   money
      b.   a customer
      c.   a product
      d.   an idea

Please go to page 140 for our relative answers and evaluation.

S. Y. N. C.

Inspirational Sayings

**Vision is seeing the opportunity
– inside the challenge**

Inspirational Sayings

Things to consider when in search of your PASSION

When life gives you lemons---
                    Make Lemonade

Life is a bowl of cherries--- Make sure you pick the right ones

So you want to be self-employed - Be Prepared, Get Prepared and Stay Prepared

Gather the pennies first -- So that soon you will be gathering your Millions

An authority is a person, who can tell you more about something, Than you really care to know!!!!!

The difference between a career and a job is about 20 hours or more A week!!!

If what you do not know doesn't kill you, it will definitely make you Stronger…

Are you in BUSINESS or just being BUSY?

If it is too good to be true, do not believe it.

H – A – L – T   Never get too Hungry - Angry - Lonely - Tired.

You cannot borrow your way into a successful business; however, You can borrow into debt.
                                        (Unknown)

THE PARADOXICAL COMMANDMENTS

Any Way

People are illogical, unreasonable, and self-centered.
Love them anyway.

If you do good, people will accuse you of selfish ulterior motives.
Do good anyway.

If you are successful, you will win false friends and true enemies.
Succeed anyway.

The good you do today will be forgotten tomorrow.
Do good anyway.

Honesty and frankness make you vulnerable.
Be honest and frank anyway.

The biggest men and women with the biggest ideas can be shot down
by the smallest men and women with the smallest minds.
Think big anyway.

People favor underdogs but follow only top dogs.
Fight for a few underdogs anyway.

What you spend years building may be destroyed overnight.
Build anyway.

People really need help but may attack you if you do help them.
Help people anyway.

Give the world the best you have and you'll get kicked in the teeth.
Give the world the best you have anyway.

S.Y.N.C. 1

Your Assessments

Rule for Success

BELIEVE IN YOURSELF

Love Thyself. Be proud of yourself. Stand tall. Of all the people on earth, there's not another person exactly like you. You are somebody, a very special person, a unique individual. Never forget that. It is most important if you are to achieve on earth what you want to achieve and what you are capable of achieving

Chapter 1

Your Assessments

Many accounting and tax preparation professionals assist individuals or groups with setting up and maintaining their small businesses. When you come to our office the first thing we want to know is information regarding your idea and your level of business knowledge. Our initial interview will allow us to gather information about your business to determine the level of care and services our office needs to provide you. We will train you and/or your staff to do the various tasks necessary to setup and maintain your business. The questions we have listed on the subsequent "Assessment # 1 Worksheet" are to assess your level of understanding of your decision to either go into business or to continue in business for yourself. You may come to us requesting assistance in determining the potential of an existing or new business venture. You may have pondered purchasing or selling a business. The possibility of owning a franchise may have fleetingly entered your mind.

We have compiled a list of questions which we feel you and/or your associates/family members may need to discuss and/or reflect upon to aid in the decision-making process of what to do in either of these scenarios.

One of the biggest reasons small businesses fail in many cases is "not knowing what you do not know".

Let me repeat this: *"You don't know what you do not know"*.

Understanding the ins and outs of your business is imperative to its success.

Many people deciding to venture into self-employment will be a first generation in their families. By not having a previous foundation and family members who may have been in business means you will be setting a fantastic precedence for your family. Performing your business activities in a profitable manner should be a top priority.

I would suggest that your very first task is to determine your present financial status. How much money does it take for me/us to live on for a week, month or year? This includes rent or mortgage, utilities, food, car expenses, beauty expenses, medical premiums and expenses, educational expenses, emergencies and climate issues. Once you have determined the budget for the family and yourself, you then need a budget for determining the breakeven point for the gross sales of your product or service. See Chapter 9 for details of breakeven points as related to your gross sales.

Prepare a list of all the items or ingredients which go into your product or service. In this list be sure to include labor, ingredients, travel, postage, printing, packaging, supplies, hired professional services, etc.

For products, write down the cost, quantity and types of all ingredients, time for preparation, packaging, equipment, gathering of the materials, shipping, marketing or pushing the product out the door for delivery.

For services, most of these industries require credentials which are verifiable through an oversight board or committee. Many of the state websites will give details as to how to obtain the proper license and credentials for the service industry you may be interested in pursuing. Examples include attorneys, doctors, beauticians, accountants, morticians, real estate brokers and many others. Refer to Chapter 15, Business Licensing, Permits, Credentials and Inspections for additional information on businesses.

Assessment Worksheet # 1

Instructions: Please write a few notes to answer each of the questions below. This will aid you in moving forward in a proper manner.

Are you a self-motivated person, self-starter, or do you usually wait on things to happen for you?

_____

_____

_____

_____

How long has this idea been brewing? Do you have notes, drawings and models to review? Have you set a time frame for your preparation?

_____

_____

_____

_____

Are you a leader or follower? List your attributes in both of these areas.

_____

_____

_____

_____

Do you have the training or education to perform your service or sell your product(s)? If not, what will it take to get the training or education of your service or product to get started?

_____

_____

_____

_____

What is the industry your product or service will focus upon? Review your industry classification at the website listed in the resource guide on page 135.

_____

_____

_____

_____

How much experience do you have in working in this industry or providing the service?

_____

_____

_____

_____

Do you have a Mentor? This is a person who has already been where you are seeking to go in business. Mentors can help you to potentially be a success in your business--some one that you can look up to and they will accept you as a friend and constituent. If you do not have a mentor, think of people you may have worked with in the industry or attempt to perform an apprenticeship under someone in the industry.

_____

_____

_____

_____

Have you created an original product or service, or is this a copy of someone else's idea? See Chapter 7 on page 42 for detail in testing the market for your product or service.

_____

_____

_____

Have you tested your market? Are your cupcakes the best in town? Possibly perform a comparison survey with other similar products or services, take a poll and analyze the results.

_____

_____

_____

_____

What is competition doing in your industry, and is your product or service something that the public would like to have?

_____

_____

_____

_____

Have you investigated the need for any trademarks or copyrights?

_____

_____

_____

_____

Does your family understand your passion, and are they willing to assist you in this venture?

_____

_____

_____

_____

How will your family help you in the beginning growth process, and is this something your family would be interested in continuing at a later date?

_____

_____

_____

_____

If you had to pick a day that your idea was conceived, please do that
now. Also, be sure to list other events which were happening around
that same time as well.

_____

_____

_____

_____

Are you a hard worker or do you wait on someone else to perform
first? How many hours do you actually work per week currently?

_____

_____

_____

_____

When you have completed this list of questions, you should be
confident and ready to start working on your new venture or ready to
review your existing on-going business activities.

Assessment Worksheet # 2

Begin by breaking your day up into either three (3-triple) or four (4-quad) sections. The three sections will represent 8 hours in each section while the four sections represent 6 hours in each section. Write down what happens in your life in each quad you choose. For example, your triple # 1 = 8 am to 4 pm: triple # 2 = 4 pm to 12 pm; and triple # 3 = 12 pm to 8 am. The boxes are presented for visual representation and reflection so you can fill your own schedule out appropriately. If you are working a full-time job, the triple times may work a little easier. Give each of these a try and remember, the important thing is to try to see where your time is going and to get as much accomplished as you can in a 24 hour day's worth of time. You can start right now by making notes on these illustrations below and in the margins.

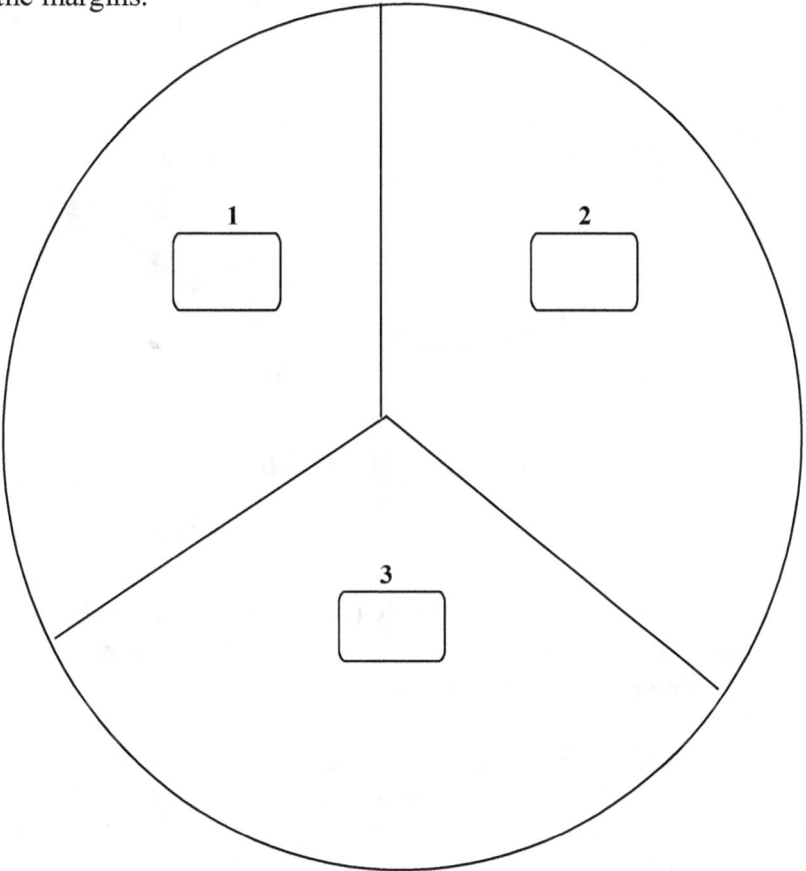

Triple - 8 Hour Sections

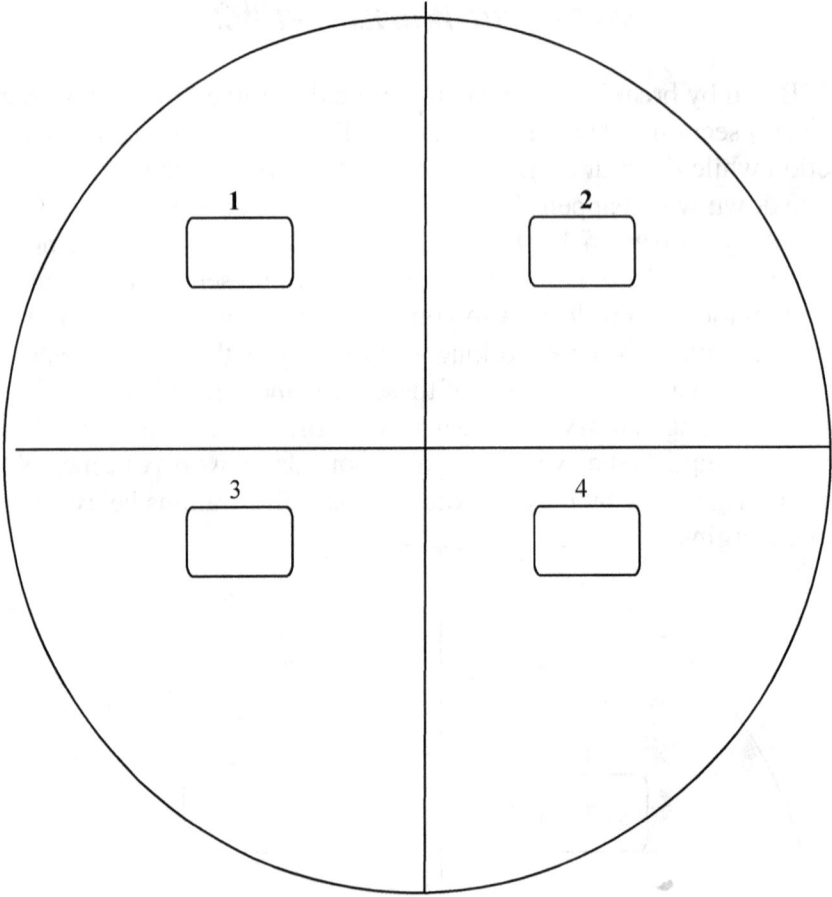

Quad – 6 Hour Sections

(Please keep in mind we all only have 24 hours in our days, unless you just invented something different, in that case no matter what time, call me first and nobody else.) ☺

Now, based on the triple and quad illustrations above, plan your sample or real daily activities. Try to remember things which you may take for granted because you either work for someone else, or your spouse takes care of these task for the family, or your parents are lonely and do not want you to leave home.

Some categories you may want to include in your listing may are:

➢ Watching TV
➢ Reading a book
➢ Quality time with the children
➢ Taking a long bath
➢ Surfing the web for research on your project
➢ Getting ready for work
➢ Cooking breakfast, lunch or dinner
➢ Going to church
➢ Providing charities with your skills and intellect
➢ Taking in a movie
➢ Watching the super bowl
➢ Baby sitting your sister's/ brother's kids
➢ Studying for an exam
➢ Going to class
➢ Sleeping

This exercise is to help you with time allocation based on time is definitely priceless. Unless your life is a constant plan of action, you first must set aside time to begin this process of becoming self-employed. With all that you already do, ask yourself how you can fit this transition into your present lifestyle.

You start by doing a little at a time. When baking a cake, you can always add a little of this or that. However, once it's in the batter, it can be difficult to take it out. ☺

Once you have assured yourself that this is what you were born for, it's time to get busy. Start out by doing in-depth research of your industry. Find out everything there is to know about your industry and determine if you have what it takes to be a part of it. If you do not have it, you must seek out how to get what you are missing and the cost which will be associated with it.

Let's say you thought you were having a dream. You and your friend see the car. You both get into the car, but your friend says "please let me drive". Your friend knows you know how to drive, so why is your friend not allowing you to drive this vehicle? You both have a few choice words about who will drive. You win the argument. You commence driving and all of a sudden your friend is shouting and acting like a crazy person in what you thought was your dream for you to wake up. You suddenly awaken to find you and your friend driving on the wrong side of the street somewhere in Europe. To say the least, you are both in the wrong seats. Going into business can be compared to a nightmare if you insist on following a particular path in your initial and growth process.

What you don't know, if it doesn't kill you, will definitely make you stronger and wiser as a small business owner. Remember to find out all you can, and then some find a little bit more, before you start your journey.

We recommend you continue working your day job until you have obtained or accumulated the proper credentials, start-up funds, the right contacts, have a mentor, have the proper wardrobe, made the commitment, worked part-time at your venture, prepared your initial business plan or mission statement and/or made it to a break-even point in your existing business venture.

This exercise is geared toward the thought process of time management. When becoming or remaining a self employed person we sometimes feel and think we have more time for ourselves. This assumption is quite the contrary, because, we really have less time to do all that we used to do and run a business. Being in business means you actually work longer and harder based on being dedicated to your passion. It means sometimes doing and going the extra mile to get the job done. At the end of the day your life and destiny are in your hands and if your time is managed well you will soar and be successful.

We welcome you to make notes on the next page for ideas which may help you latter in your brain storming sessions.

NOTES

S.Y.N.C. 2

Appointment Book or Scheduler

Rule for Success

REACH FOR THE STARS

Set high standards and seek with
all your energies to reach them. A
very famous Chicago advertising
executive, Leo Burnett, who died
not long ago, said something like,
"Reach for the stars, and while you
may never quite catch one, you
will never come up with a handful
of mud." And that's good advice
for each of us. So keep your sights
high and your standards high – and
that will help you achieve more
than you think possible in your
lifetime.

Chapter 2

Appointment Book or Scheduler

How will you keep up with yourself and your family?

An appointment book or calendar is of great importance in keeping track of all that goes into getting your project up and running, but also will aid in documenting many other kinds of information which will assist you through your initial stages and down the road.

This is an excellent way to document time, effort, money, travel, and the research you have invested in your project over a period of time. As you go through the initial stages of setting up your business, you may not realize just what you have invested until you need to account for this information later. Many of these items may or will have monetary and income tax rewards for you if you are able to document them as you go. Keeping up with the meetings, copying, faxing, research materials, contacts and your journey will also assist when you are ready to prepare the narrative or history of your business plan.

In today's standards an appointment book or scheduler may be maintained by a variety of devices both manually and electronically. If you start using one method and feel the need to make a change, do not be alarmed or frustrated, just be consistent. Many people have multiple ways of keeping track of their businesses and family matters. Whatever works for you is the correct one to use. There are various calendar products on line and at the supply store. Please visit our Resources Guide on chapter 20, page 135 for a quick link to an online calendar resource. In some cases certain individuals will have both an electronic and a hardcopy appointment book to keep their lives in sync.

In some cases setting up your electronic calendar in your email software can be of great benefit. Your contacts and other information will all be in one place. There are several electronic email, calendar and contact programs available. This software will allow you to import and export to an excel spreadsheet your notes and everything you enter into your scheduler, as well as, allow you to print a hard copy if necessary for your accountant. By saving your data in an organized manner, you may be able to include some items as documentation in the preparation of your income tax returns. Most of these software programs will at some point want to archive your data, so we recommend exporting and labeling a worksheet for a specific period of time, just in case you need to refer to your important information later. Having notes to include results from meetings and events will also validate the event and any deductibility questions of the transaction.

It would be nice if at some point your notes can be converted to either an electronic or digital format for your future reference and to allow you to eliminate the need to maintain the paper trail for an extended long-term period of time. However, do not toss the paper trail until you have completed your project or income taxes--just make it a part of your master recordkeeping system.

Your scheduler should keep up with your meetings designed to gather, share, sell or confirm information regarding your product or service. These notes should include all the names of the parties at the meeting, the place and time, as well as brief notes regarding the discussion. Also, it is to your benefit to use your scheduler as a means of keeping up with expenses, logging mileage and reminders regarding purchases made for the day, so when your accountant asks why an item was purchased, you will be able to answer intelligently and your accountant can properly code the transaction in your books of record. In today's world where time is of the essence, maintaining family agendas is equally as important as the business aspects; and sometimes the two will meet or cross over.

You may even need to assign some tasks you previously performed to another family member so you can work on various ways of making your business more successful. Keep in mind there are tax benefits for hiring your family and/or your spouse.

Involving your family in your new business venture will definitely inspire them to help you. It may even lead them to earning a few extra dollars, which you can write off as an expense, and still get some things accomplished. This tax loophole is one that is often overlooked or not taken advantage of because most people don't have this book. Hiring your children or spouse will save thousands of dollars in income tax obligations and give them a spirited sense of just what you do and should yield a positive end result with them. One thing is for sure; your children won't make the same mistakes you do because you will have paved the road to success for them. They may even eventually come up with their own ideas and projects.

Included are sample hard copies of schedulers for you to use on pages 32 and 33. A few items which definitely should be listed are things to do, meetings, purchases and other items to include:

- Researching your product or services.
- Asking how much education I need to perform my task, manufacture and sell my product or services.
- Testing my product or services to see if this is something that I will have ready for the market or buyer.
- Time to work on my business plan.
- Scheduling meeting with your team members and staff.

Schedule weekly/monthly/quarterly family meetings, and do not overlook the financial part of the family at this time. These meetings should include updates on everyone's life. This allows you to take a minute for no expectations, but to involve each other and comingle your lives. These meetings should not be scheduled during holidays, birthdays, death or other special occasions. Remember, these are business-oriented meetings with personal time comingled. Don't forget food for the socialization. Please visit our Resources Guide located in Chapter 20, page 135 for a website of free printable calendars.

Weekly Schedule 12.01.XXXX to 12.07.XXXX

Sunday 12.01. This page may be copied for your use. xxxx	11.00 am - Church or spiritual renewal. 2.00 pm Dinner with family and hold family meeting to update status of all family members. 6.00 pm - Spend one hour working on product cost and breakeven points revenues. Be in bed no later than 10.00 pm.
Monday 12.02.xxxx	
Tuesday 12.03.xxxx	11.00 am Meet with prospective Accountant. Remember to log your mileage to and from for later calculations
Wednesday 12.04.xxxx	Contact five (5) Office Centers for company meetings and market my services.
Thursday 12.05.xxxx	Purchased Cannon Camera $ 995.26. Used VISA # 2275 — Represents last 4 digits of CC used for purchase
Friday 12.06.xxxx	9.30 am Meet with prospective Attorney DXXXX.
Saturday 12.07.xxxx	9 am to 12 pm - Seminar on how to speak and greet potential customers. How to close the sale. Cost: $75.00, including lunch.

Notes:_____

S.Y.N.C. - This page may be copied for your use.

Weekly Schedule _____ to _____

Sunday	
Monday	
Tuesday	
Wednesday	
Thursday	
Friday	
Saturday 12.07.xxxx	

Notes:_____

Monthly Calendar_____

Sun	Mon	Tue	Wed	Thu	Fri	Sat

Notes:_____

_____

S.Y.N.C. 3

Narrative of the History of Business Idea from the Beginning

Rule for Success

HONOR AND RESPECT

YOUR PARENTS

They've worked and sweated and
prayed for you. You may think
they're old fashioned and out of
touch, not with it, not so cool.
But they're your parents, and they
deserve your love and respect.
Whatever you become, they will
deserve a great deal of the credit
and thanks.

Chapter 3

Narrative of the History of Business Idea from the Beginning

This is where you are able to write whatever you feel, think or desire. This is about you, who you were and potentially who you will become as a result of your unyielding quest for success as a small business owner. My sample narrative may begin as follows:

As a youth, I was always very inquisitive--lots of questions and "why's". My parents had a store and when I was just toddler and I remember having whatever I wanted at my fingertips. Let us fast forward a few years. Being empowered by not only one but two school teachers, my mom and dad, I decided that I had to do a few things on my own. Growing up in the south held a unique and special set of experiences". This is a short sample of a narrative as prepared by the author.

Business narratives are creative exercises designed as a pre-cursor to a formalized business proposal. The purpose of a business narrative is to allow you to organize and express your business ideas freely and creatively. Elements of your business narrative can even be used to draft to compose your final, formal business proposal. Writing a business narrative requires you to brainstorm and organize your preliminary business ideas before piecing them together in a cohesive story.

Instructions

1. Prepare and plan for your business narrative. We suggest brainstorming about your business idea for at least 15 to 30 minutes a day and writing about everything, including product production, staffing, management, location, target audience, concerns, problems, obscene matters, family thoughts and competitors. Be sure to gather all of your notes, email correspondence and even doodles you've naturally generated while mulling over your business idea or just simple expression.

All these little items will eventually become a part of your final product analysis, detailing your business narrative.

2. Gather recurring ideas about your business into a list format. We emphasize the importance of key terms, phrases and concepts related to your business idea; while we encourage you to focus on the recurring problems you experienced that inspired you to dream up your business idea.

3. Highlight recurring themes, trends, phrases, ideas, terms, problems and solutions in your assembled notes. These concepts will likely become crucial components of your future business narrative.

4. Develop a name for your business based upon your initial idea, as well as the highlighted concepts from your brainstorming activities. The named business will be the central figure or "character" of your narrative. If you are struggling to develop a name for the business, give your business a generic name, but don't forget to fill in your chosen name later.

5. Craft a description of what your business does and why it is unlike any other business. Begin each sentence with action words, such as "prepare," "gather," "highlight," "provide", "develop" and "craft."

6. Identify the specific market and customers that will be served by your business and the specific needs of the customers your product or service will address.

7. Describe your business goals and the different resources and actions you will need to accomplish those goals. Qualify each required resource or action with a description of how you will acquire or accomplish it.

8. Conclude your narrative with a description of why you are confident your business will succeed. We believe you should draw parallels between yourself and other business leaders and your business model and other successful businesses in the world.

9. Assemble your business narrative. We recommend a simple format, in which you introduce and describe your main character (business name), which is then confronted with a challenging quest (business goals), including obstacles the character (business) must overcome (reaching the specific market and customers) and how it achieves success. Other narrative ideas include a parable that aligns your business plan with other successful business ventures, identifying the similarities between the two, and a biography, which follows you through the formulation, development and nurturing of your business plan.

10. The actual type of company narrative/biography will be determined based on the audience you are addressing. Just like when you are seeking employment with a company, your resume may accentuate a particular skill or credential, your business narrative/biography should vary as well, depending upon to whom you are presenting your information: i.e. Banker, Customer, Investor, etc..

Observe the World

The greatest ideas appear when you least expect them. Sit in the park and watch the world unfold around you. Who walks by? What do they look like? How do they interact with others? Take notes, consider the meaning of their actions, and begin to let your imagination wander. People-watching can be a fantastic way to gain inspiration and develop ideas for a narrative piece. Remember to observe and take note of details of the world around you.

S.Y.N.C. 4

Resumes/Biographies

Rule for Success

DO SOMETHING FOR SOMEBODY ELSE

No matter how hard or bleak your
own life may seem, there are plenty
of others worse off. So find a way to
help, even one person. Your life will
be richer for it.

Chapter 4

Resumes/Biographies

Resumes/Biographies are perhaps the most important features and tools you will use to obtain what you want as a new business owner to present to your prospective buyers and/or investors. All good business plans include a personal resume of all individuals involved in the venture or project. These readers will be interested in knowing your background in relationship to the business you plan to pursue. Essentially, you are advertising for a new and exciting position in your own company.

If you are in an existing business, the resumes of all key personnel should be included in this section

A "COMPANY" resume is also beneficial to include in this section. For start-up companies, explain the concept and what brought you to the stage where you are now pursuing company contracts, investors, large corporate buyers or financing.

1. Choose one or two fonts at most, and avoid underlined, boldfaced and italic text. Many prospective readers of your resume / bio will be anxious to quickly see who you are and what you may want of them.

2. Opt for the active voice, rather than the passive.

3. Provide contact information such as your address, phone number, e-mail address and website at the top of your resume. Try to purchase your name as a domain so that when you become more successful someone will not try to sell it back to you.

4. Include an objectives statement, in which you use clear, simple language to indicate what you are looking for from the reader. This should appear directly below your contact information.

5. Prepare a list of your most recent and relevant experience first. Include time frames, company names and job titles, followed by major responsibilities. If you have been preparing research for

your project which has been exciting and eventful, you may want to include a snippet of that information here to achieve a greater interest in your mission.

6. In a second section, outline your education, credentials, awards, accomplishments and anything else you wish the prospective readers to know about you.

7. Hire a proofreader or have someone you trust to proofread your resume as well as your business plan. Mistakes in spelling, grammar or syntax can be a real turnoff to the reader, whether they be a potential investor or purchaser of your products or services.

8. Limit your resume/bio to one page unless it is scientific or highly technical. Less is definitely more when it comes to this type of introduction of you.

9. Be specific and detail oriented when describing yourself and your goals.

10. The actual type of company resume/biography will be determined based on the audience you are addressing. Just like when you are seeking employment with a company, your resume may accentuate a particular skill or credential, your personal resume/biography should vary as well, depending upon to whom you are presenting your information: i.e. Banker, Customer, Investor, etc.

Sample Resume Format

Your Contact Information
First Last Name
Street Address
City, State, Zip
Phone (Cell/Home)
Email Address

Objective / Mission Statement
What do you want to do? If you include this section it should be a sentence or two about your employment goals. A customized objective that describes why you are the perfect candidate for the job can help your resume stand out from the competition.

Career Highlights / Qualifications
A customized section of your resume that lists key achievements, skills, traits, and experience relevant to the position for which you are applying can serve dual purposes. It highlights your relevant experience and lets the prospective employer know that you have taken the time to create a resume that shows how you are qualified for the job.

Experience
This section of your resume includes your work history. List the companies you worked for, dates of employment, the positions you held and a bulleted list of responsibilities and achievements.

Company #1   **Telephone Number**
Company Address
City, State Zip Code

Dates Worked
Job Title
- Responsibilities / Achievements
- Responsibilities / Achievements

Company #2   **Telephone Number**
Company Address
City, State Zip Code

Dates Worked
Job Title
- Responsibilities / Achievements
- Responsibilities / Achievements

Education
In the education section of your resume, list the schools you attended, the degrees you attained, and any special awards and honors you earned. Colleges or Universities, Degrees, Awards, Honors, Certificates

Skills: Include skills related to the position / career field that you are applying for i.e. computer skills, language skills.

References available upon request:
There is no need to include references on your resume. Rather, have a separate list of references to give to readers upon request.

S.Y.N.C. 5

Developing Your Vision

Rule for Success

ALWAYS DO A LITTLE MORE THAN YOU'RE EXPECTED TO DO

Don't try to get away with a little less. When you're assigned a chore by your teacher, your employer, your mother or father, go the extra mile, even the extra foot. Do a little more. They will notice and be grateful, and such an attitude will bring you great satisfaction and big dividends.

Chapter 5

Developing Your Vision

Review the research, training and development of your product or service passion or idea

The idea of your product or service may have been conceived in your youth. The idea may have come as a result of a teacher, a method, a family vacation, inspired by a family member, reading a book or magazine or just in the midst of performing a task that you felt could be improved upon. However the idea came about, you now have it and it has become your passion. Once you know your passion you can begin the ground work for building your successful business. The end result will be to gain personal satisfaction, make money and launch your family to a higher financial independence.

Do you have a great idea for a business service and/or product? The primary reason for launching a new business is being inspired by an entrepreneurial idea. However, before putting a major investment of your time, energy and money into your venture, experts suggest you conduct some test marketing to decide whether or not a new product/service is worthy of pursuit.

How can you prepare for test marketing?

A good test market will include a marketing plan to reveal those customers most likely to buy your product / service, and on whom you can concentrate your test-marketing efforts.

– 4 Questions to Ask Yourself –

1.   What are the reasons potential customers would want to purchase my product or service? Have participants complete a brief survey.

2.   What does my product/service have that my competitor's don't?

3.   Does my idea follow a short-term trend or one with a potential long-term future?

4.   Is my product/service cost-effective and likely to produce profits needed to sustain a thriving business?

– 8 Affordable Test Marketing Methods –

1.   If you have a product, give away samples to friends and family members, or at flea markets and trade shows. Ask for immediate and honest feedback.

2.   If you have a service idea, perform your service for free for family, friends or non-profit organizations to see if you are good enough at it to make money.

3.   Run classified ads, give out fliers, or send out a direct mailing with a (postage paid) survey card to see what kind of response you receive in terms of orders and/or requests for your services.

4.   Send out a quarterly promotional newsletter with a questionnaire asking customers to evaluate not only new products and/or services, but your existing ones.

5.   Send press releases to print, radio and television media announcing the release of your new product and/or services in conjunction with a contest or giveaway promotion.

6.   Contact high school or business college classes to see if they will conduct valuable consumer research for you gratis, as a class project.

7.   Team up with an established business owner to offer your product and/or services as an additional sideline to their venture.

8.   Make telephone calls to interested companies or individuals, (or/and conduct polls among people who have indicated they would like more information about your business). Be sure you are aware of the "Do Not Call" rules and include a waiver statement on your materials if you think you should.

– 4 Ways to Evaluate the Results –

1. How many people liked your idea and/or product and said they would definitely buy or use it?

2. Did your efforts result in new customers and/or revenues from orders?

3. Did you discover a new market area?

4. If you had a poor response in your community, is there a nearby location better suited to your idea?

Conducting thorough test marketing will help guide you in making strategic business decisions, and make it more likely you'll become a successful entrepreneur.

When you have set your personal goals, you should then project your revenues and expenses for the next three years along with strategic breakeven points. Once you have estimated the cost and resources, you will then have the commitment that will be necessary for you to generate these projections, and you are ready to develop your plans for growth. Imagine having an order for 10,000 units and not having a manufacturer to provide them for you to sell.

First, you should delineate the four areas of your business that you believe would yield the greatest returns for the expenditure of time and money. These become your **strategies** for growth. Strategies are the activities that you believe will yield the greatest return on time and money spent in advancing you to your goals.

Next you should estimate the amount of time and effort you are willing to commit on a weekly basis for working on the strategies or activities that you have identified. These become your **commitments** and should be identified on your commitment sheet. You should also determine how much you are worth in the process of managing, working and overseeing your business operations. We recommend you consider the amount of your current hourly pay rate, if you are employed, before deductions, multiplied by a factor of 1½ times, for starters. As the business grows and you take on more responsibility, this factor may be increased to 2 or 3 times your original earnings rate. Remember if you do not get paid, nobody else gets paid either.

Once you have ascertained that you have a product or service which the mass public would like to purchase, you need to determine if you need a trademark, patent or copyright to protect the success of your company. This too is a part of your research which protects you from another company or person illegally taking possession of your idea. The following definitions will put you on the path for a little more research which could prove to be invaluable later for your business success.

Trademarks

Distinctive symbols of authenticity through which the products of particular manufacturers or the salable commodities of particular merchants can be distinguished from those of others. (United States Patent and Trademark Office)

A trademark is a device, word or combination of words, or symbol that indicates the source or ownership of a product or service. A trademark can be a name, such as Adidas, or a symbol, such as McDonald's golden arches, or it can be a combination of the two, such as when the NIKE name is written with the "swoosh" symbol beneath it. In very limited cases, a shape or even a distinctive color can become a trademark.

People rely on trademarks to make informed decisions about the products they buy. A trademark acts as a guarantee of the quality and origin of a particular good. A competing manufacturer may not use another company's trademark. The owner of a trademark may challenge any use of the mark that infringes upon the owner's rights.

The presence of trademark protection for the name or logo of a company or product is often indicated by the small symbol of an R in a circle placed near the trademark. The R means that the mark is a registered trademark and is a warning that the law prevents unauthorized use of it. A party may indicate that it is claiming rights to a particular mark by displaying a TM rather than an R symbol. Marks bearing the TM symbol are not registered, but the presence of the symbol shows intent to register.

Traditionally, trademark rights had depended on prior use, but since 1988 a party with a genuine intent to use a mark may apply for trademark registration. The applicant must intend to use the mark in commerce and must intend to do so in order to sell a product, not merely to reserve rights for future use.

Patents

Rights, granted to inventors by the federal government, pursuant to its power under Article I, Section 8, Clause 8, of the U.S. Constitution, that permit them to exclude others from making, using, or selling an invention for a definite, or restricted, period of time. (United States Patent and Trademark Office)

The U.S. patent system is designed to encourage inventions that are useful to society by granting inventors the absolute right to exclude all others from using or profiting from their invention for a limited time, in exchange for disclosing the details of the invention to the public. Once a patent has expired, the public then has the right to make, use, or sell the invention.

Once a patent is granted, it is regarded as the "Personal Property" of the inventor. An inventor's property rights in an invention itself are freely transferable and assignable. Often employees who invent something in the course and scope of their employment transfer and assign their property rights in the invention to their employer. In addition, a patent holder, or patentee, can grant a license to another to use the invention in exchange for payment or a royalty.

Inventors are not required to participate in the patent system, and they can elect instead to try to keep their invention a trade secret. However, if the inventor begins to sell his or her invention or allows the public to use it, others can study the invention and create impostor products. If this happens, the original inventor has no protection because he or she did not obtain a patent.

There are three types of patents: (1) design patents, (2) plant patents, and (3) utility patents. Design patents are granted to protect a unique appearance or design of an article of manufacture, whether it is surface ornamentation or the overall configuration of an object. Plant patents are granted for the invention and asexual reproduction of a new and distinct variety of plant, including mutants and hybrids.

Utility patents are perhaps the most familiar, applying to machines, chemicals, and processes.

One important change in U.S. patent law resulting from GATT is the duration of U.S. patents. Patents were originally given 14-year terms from the date of issue, until that was changed in 1861. From 1861 until the implementation of GATT, the term of a patent was 17 years from the date of issue. Under GATT, all patents issued after June 7, 1995, have a term of 20 years from the effective filing date. GATT contained a retroactive component which provided that all patents that had been issued, but not yet expired, as of June 7, 1995, would have a term that is the longer of 20 years from its effective filing date or 17 years from the date of issue. The effective filing date is the date on which the earliest U.S. application is filed under which priority is claimed. In the United States, patent rights begin when the patent is issued.

Copyright

A bundle of intangible rights granted by statute to the author or originator of certain literary or artistic productions, whereby, for a limited period, the exclusive privilege is given to that person (or to any party to whom he or she transfers ownership) to make copies of the same for publication and sale. (United States Patent and Trademark Office)

A copyright is a legal device that gives the creator of a literary, artistic, musical, or other creative work the sole right to publish and sell that work. Copyright owners have the right to control the reproduction of their work, including the right to receive payment for that reproduction. An author may grant or sell those rights to others, including publishers or recording companies. Violation of a copyright is called infringement.

Copyright is distinct from other forms of creator protection such as **Patents**, which give inventors exclusive rights over use of their inventions, and **Trademarks**, which are legally protected words or symbols or certain other distinguishing features that represent products or services. Similarly, whereas a patent protects the application of an idea, and a trademark protects a device that indicates the provider of particular services or goods, copyright protects the expression of an idea. Whereas the operative notion in patents is novelty, so that a patent represents some invention that is new and has never been made before, the basic concept behind copyright is originality, so that a copyright represents something that has originated from a particular author and not from another. Copyrights, patents, and trademarks are all examples of what is known in the law as Intellectual Property.

As the media on which artistic and intellectual works are recorded have changed with time, a copyright protection has been extended from the printing of text to many other means of recording original expressions. Besides books, stories, periodicals, poems, and other printed literary works, copyright may protect computer programs; musical compositions; song lyrics; dramas; dramatic-musical compositions; pictorial, graphic, and sculptural works; architectural works; written directions for pantomimes and choreographic works; motion pictures and other audiovisual works; and sound recordings.

S.Y.N.C. 6

Gather Your Team to Aid in Your Quest

Rule for Success

BE TRUE TO YOURSELF

Be honest with yourself. This means being honest even when it hurts. This means doing the right thing even when nobody's watching. You may be able to kid most people, but you can never really fool yourself. If you set high standards for yourself, and generally stick to them, then you are being true to yourself. Few who betray themselves ever really succeed.

Chapter 6

Gather Your Team to Aid in Your Quest

As by now you are aware, we are here to assist you avoiding many, if any, serious mistakes in your journey to being a successful small business owner. As with anything, no man or woman is an island; it takes a village to raise a child, and trust trumps flattery.

Once you are dedicated to your journey, you will encounter quite a few people and organizations who will want to inadvertently share information or encourage you to purchase their products or services. The list of team persons below are by no means all-inclusive but should assist you with your major players.

We recommend you set up interviews with persons in all the categories listed below. Many companies welcome this mode of interviewing to assist their companies in obtaining new business. Most of your professional service vendors may allow anywhere from 15–30 minutes of free consultation and entertain questions, review your needs or particular concerns you may have. Others may charge a nominal fee, but I say pay the fee, get what you need (information to determine if you want to hire their company) and move on to the next interview.

Keep in mind that way down the road you are going to transition from this initial business possibly into something else or a different idea altogether. Therefore, having key resources with personable association is paramount to your success in this business right from the beginning and your future endeavors.

Be prepared with your list of questions and note paper or a recording device, of course with the permission of the interviewed, and be sure to listen. You are not there for a job interview; you are there as a prospective employer of this person and their firm. The conference could require only a brief phone call or, if your venture has complexities, more time and abilities may be required.

The following is a prospective list of individuals and resources we recommend you should have on board to hopefully assure yourself of a successful team.

1. Accountant

2. Attorney
3. Banker and other Financial Resources
4. Financial Planner
5. Real Estate Broker
6. Staffing

You should seek the abilities of qualified professionals in these disciplines if you plan on investing in or selling a business, buying or selling real estate, refinancing assets, or entering into other arrangements which involve legal, accounting, tax, insurance or financial matters.

Accountant

Good recordkeeping services, tax advice, preparation of tax returns, accounting, management advisory services and general business counseling are among the services offered by the professional accountant. They should be available at a fair and reasonable fee.

Accountants are normally licensed by a Board of Accountancy in their respective states. They are required to meet a specific level of continuing education requirements and are overseen by a regulatory board. When interviewing your accountant, ask for a list of their credentials or a biography to review their background information. Our office does not "Name Drop" current clients; however, obtaining a referral from someone of an Accountant may be the way to go. Keep in mind with all referrals, each case is different and the person making the referral may not have or need the same business expertise and financial consulting matters you are seeking for your new or existing business venture.

You may want to consider hiring a bookkeeper for your day-to-day operations. When interviewing this person or company, make sure the prospective person has certain office skills. These skills will assist you in making sound financial decisions for the success of your company. Some of these skills may include fluency with staff, financial institutions, computer spreadsheets, office task such as scanning documents and coordinating documents either manually or via electronic means for ease of accessing and processing.

Like many other professionals, the accountant does not sell a product, but rather renders a service.

It is natural for the prospective client or the existent client, in all industries, interested in some new service to be concerned about the cost of those services to be rendered. So it is with the professional accountant, where fees must always be reasonable for the practice to endure.

At the heart of every fee is the training and experience the accountant brings to the client's particular accounting or tax issue. Knowledgeable of changes in tax and regulations, as well as newly developing principles of accounting, the accountant must be able to serve clients in an up-to-date, competent manner.

One of the more important discussions you will have during the tenure of your client/accountant relationship will be on the accountant's method of charging for their services.

In your first visit to the accountant whose services you wish to retain, by all means engage in a clear discussion of the fees to be charged. Your accountant would want it this way so that you both will have full understanding as to the nature of the services you wish performed. Never hesitate to sit down with your accountant and discuss how the fees are set in your particular case.

The professional accountant's fees are important to both the client and the accountant. Many times the fee for a given type of service will be found to be very close to the customary charges for similar services in a given locale. But, since no two situations are ever exactly alike, the fee structure for any two engagements will rarely if ever be exactly the same.

Some major factors when choosing your accountant...

If you have never utilized the services of the professional practicing accountant, you may be interested in learning of some of the major factors going into the make-up of a fee, such as:

1. Time—time is important and constitutes a major ingredient in fee structuring. Many accountants keep exact records of the time they expend on a particular client's projects—the time of the principal accountant, their assistants, clerical or support staff as may be necessary in a complex assignment, or perhaps the time of just one accountant in a less complex situation—and fees are established based on the amount of time expended for the engagement. Our firm uses stop watches to track our time to the second. We then record our time spent, date task was performed and a description of what was done.

2. Degree of skill involved—not all engagements necessitating a high or moderately-high degree of skill require a substantial amount of time. But they do bring into play special skills which are time consuming, acquired by background and experience, and which demand higher fees than do tasks of a lesser degree of skill. The preparation of tax returns for a complex business or personal situation is one example of this.

3. Duration and nature of the engagement—obviously, the length of time from start to completion, as well as the nature of the assignment, are important to both the client and the accountant, requiring the scheduling of staff resources and the melding of priorities and staff commitments.

4. Unusual or especially difficult situations—these require special planning, presenting a complexity over and above that which would be present in the normal situation. This in itself would probably necessitate a fee adjustment in excess of the norm.

Taking each of these factors into consideration during the client/accountant discussions referred to above, the accountant will often be able to provide the client with a general idea of the approximate fee which will be involved in the particular assignment.

In this, as in many human endeavors involving others, there are three things which invariably make for improvement or success: discussion, understanding and mutual agreement

Attorney

The United States has more lawyers per person than any other country. So, if you need one--and many of us do at one time or another--you should be able to find one who will provide the best professional counsel at the fairest price.

This section outlines how to decide if, in fact, you need the services of a lawyer and, if so, how to select one. It also offers some important tips on working with a lawyer to get the most out of every dollar you spend on legal advice.

1. When to Look for Legal Advice -- When seeking an attorney be sure to inquire of their dealings with small businesses. Some attorneys will specialize only in business matters. We believe it is better to have an attorney available and who has accepted you as a client. Then, if the need should arise, you are not in the midst of dealing with an issue and trying to find help. Although many problems can be resolved without involving a lawyer, in this case it is better to have one and not need one, then to need one and can't find one. The questions and answers similar to those listed below can help you decide whether you need legal help.

> *Can I handle this problem myself?*
> *Where can I go if I cannot afford legal fees, but need a lawyer's help?*

2. How to Select a Lawyer

- Begin by asking friends, neighbors, or co-workers about lawyers they have used. Pay special attention to what you hear from people who have had problems like yours that were resolved in a satisfactory way.

- Contact your state, city, or county bar association and ask for the names and phone numbers of lawyers who handle cases within your area of concern. Most bar associations have a Lawyer Referral and Information Service to provide this kind of information.

- Check the Yellow Pages for areas of specialty, hours and locations. You also may obtain information by looking for lawyer advertisements in newspapers and on the radio and television.

- If you live or work near a law school, contact the dean's office, describe your problem, and ask if the school or individual faculty members are able to recommend someone to take your case.

Here are a few questions to ask your attorney about the services to be provided:

Will you meet with me to get acquainted before I hire you?
What percentage of your practice is devoted to cases like mine?
Will you personally work on my case, or will you delegate it to an associate or paralegal assistant?
Will you keep me notified about the progress of my case?
How long should it take you to complete my case and what, roughly, is it going to cost me?
If something goes wrong between us, will you consent to binding arbitration?

3. Negotiating Fees-- Most fees are agreed upon through discussions between clients and lawyers. If you cannot afford what the lawyer asks, say so. Fees *are* negotiable. Shop around until you find a lawyer who is willing to work within your budget. If necessary, you may want to discuss working out a payment plan if you do not think you can afford a lump fee.

Here are some questions to ask about fees:

What services do you provide for a flat fee?
What are your hourly rates?
Do you require a retainer for your services?
Do you accept contingency fee arrangements?

The best way to protect yourself and avoid misunderstandings is to have the agreement you make with your lawyer put into writing and signed by both parties. A request to put your agreement in writing should be made at the first meeting between you and your lawyer, before your lawyer begins any work on your case.

Banker and Other Financial Resources

The bank and the banker are not one in the same. Once you have decided on the bank you would like to use for conducting your business and financial transactions, you now need to find a banker to assist you when and if the time arises. A competent banker can be one of your best resources to assist with the growth and success of your business.

Open a checking account with a friendly personable bank manager or loan officer to establish a sound long-term business banking relationship.

- Be confident, enthusiastic and well prepared.
- Determine if you need a smaller or larger bank for your goals and banking needs.

Branch offices are also important to determine accessibility. If your business takes you away from your local area, check to see if your bank of choice has locations in other areas. Also, ask if they provide international banking.

In some cases, you've just become familiar with your banker, and then the bank transfers them to a different branch or department. At this point you need to choose someone else or follow your original banker, if the relationship is strong. Many bank managers have the ability to lend funds up to a certain limit without going to the board. This could be helpful for short-term funds when your business is growing and you have orders to fill.

Be sure to review our "Business Banking Process Information" in Chapter 13 on page 96 for details of setting up your business bank account.

Financial Planner

Today, nearly a quarter of a million American men and women earn their living as financial planners. If you decide to hire a financial planner, a good one should analyze your finances and recommend how to improve your financial situation. Successful financial planners may have as many different investment strategies as the clients they serve. Make sure the financial planner you choose works on behalf of your interests and needs.

Since you are self-employed you are eligible for specific tax deferral plans. SEP, SIMPLE, and qualified plans offer you and your employees a tax-favored way to save for retirement. You can deduct contributions you make to the plan for your employees. If you are a sole proprietor, you can deduct contributions you make to the plan for yourself. You can also deduct trustees' fees if contributions to the plan do not cover them. Earnings on the contributions are generally tax free until you or your employees receive distributions from the plan.

A financial planner should assist you in the following ways:

- Assess your relevant financial history, such as tax returns, investments, retirements plan, wills, and insurance policies.
- Help you decide on a financial plan, based on your personal and financial goals, history, and preferences.
- Identify financial areas where you may need help, such as building up a retirement income or improving your investment returns.
- Write down a financial plan based on your individual situation and discuss it thoroughly with you in plain English.
- Help you implement your financial plan, including referring you to specialists, such as lawyers or accountants, if necessary.
- Review your situation and financial plan periodically and suggest changes in your program when needed.

Before you select a financial planner, you may want to ask yourself these questions:

What are my financial goals today and ten years from now?
What is my personal investment philosophy?
What credentials do you have to practice financial planning?
How would you prepare my financial plan?
How many companies do you represent?
Who will I deal with on a regular basis?
How do you keep up with the latest financial developments?
Will you be involved in implementing the plan you suggest?

Be sure to question financial planners carefully about their background and experience. Be wary of individuals who promote various investment items without discussing with you any overall financial planning goals. They may lack the expertise to formulate one.

Are you registered with the federal Securities and Exchange Commission (SEC) or with a state agency?

Negotiating Financial Planner Fees

Fee arrangements with a financial planner are quite similar to the payment system for a lawyer. There are a variety of fee options that you should explore to see which serves your interest best. Ask about the following arrangements:

1. **Fee-only Financial Planners** base their charge on gathering your financial data, analyzing it, and recommending a plan of action. Hourly or flat fees are most common. Payment is required *whether or not* you choose to implement the suggested plan. Many fee-only planners cater to wealthy investors, but you may try this arrangement if you can negotiate a reasonable price.

2. **Commission-only Planners** charge no fee for service to their client but make their money instead through commissions paid by the marketers of the investment products they sell. For example, if a client buys insurance on the advice of a financial planner, the planner will not charge the client for that advice but will receive a commission from the insurance company.

Planners who rely only on commissions might be more eager to direct your financial plan toward the purchase of products that provide them with the best commissions. Therefore, you may want to exercise caution in following the advice of a planner who works on commission until you develop a trusting relationship with one who knows your complete financial picture.

3. **Fee and Commission Planners** receive payments from both a sales commission and a fee. If, for example, the planner receives a commission from the company that sells the product you purchase, the fee you are charged may be less.

Written Estimate of Fees and Services

Make sure you get a written estimate of what services you can expect for what price. Compare this estimate with others and select the package of services that best meets your needs.

Real Estate Broker

If you are selling or buying a home, or interested in a commercial piece of real estate, you may want to consider using a real estate broker. Although you are not required to use a broker, many consumers do. Real estate brokers may be able to provide information about real estate values, financing, and standard sales agreements. In addition, a realtor may be able to assist you in locating an excellent location for your business as well. The following information may help you decide whether you want to work with one and, if you do, what services and terms you may want to arrange.

You can find real estate brokers through friends, advertisements, and the Yellow Pages. Both real estate "brokers" and real estate "Salespersons" are licensed by the state, but salespersons must be supervised by brokers. The term "broker" here refers to both groups, but keep in mind that you actually may be dealing with the broker's salesperson.

Before selecting a real estate broker to help you, you first may want to interview brokers from several firms. Ask them to provide you with the names and phone numbers of previous clients, if possible, to call as references.

For many people, leasing business real estate makes good financial sense. Often leasing means a smaller cash outlay and more flexibility than buying. If you are considering leasing, evaluate the following factors:

Location

For most businesses, the location for customer access can either make or break you. Will the building meet your current and future space requirements? Does the location have enough parking for your customers, employees and delivery vehicles?

If there are other tenants on the premises, are their business operations compatible with yours? Also check the landlord's track record concerning repairs and maintenance.

Is the property currently zoned for your business requirements, and are there any pending zoning changes which will affect the desirability of the location?

Cost

The cost of a lease is usually broken down into the cost per square foot. To determine the true cost, you should understand the difference between rental (total) space and usable (revenue-producing) space. You should also be familiar with the terms "gross" and "net." Under a gross lease, the landlord pays for insurance, property taxes, utilities and maintenance. Under a net lease, you pay.

If alterations have to be made to the property, agree in writing who is paying, how much and for what.

Options

Various options can be included in the lease to ensure flexibility. The usual options cover renewal, subleasing and eventual purchase by the tenant and cancellation by either party.

A lease is a binding legal agreement. Your attorney should draft or review the document before you commit to any terms.

Staffing

As you begin your business operating activity you may require assistants who have certain skills to help you with tasks. When you decide to expand to include more personnel there are several options available to you. We will define two options below to help you understand your responsibility as a small business owner as directly related to your staffing requirements.

Independent Contractor

The general rule is that an individual is an independent contractor if the payer has the right to control or direct _only_ the results of the work and not what will be done and how it will be performed to get to the end result, the individual's financial control over their own profit or loss and the relationship of the parties. The earnings of a person who is working as an independent contractor are subject to Self-Employment Tax. You will be required to submit to this individual a Form 1099-Misc Non-Employee Compensation, at the end of the year if you pay them more than $600.00 for the year. The contractor is also responsible for maintaining their records to reconcile with your records at the end of the year. Regulations for contract persons have changed recently. It is your responsibility to be abreast of new and pending tax regulations for contractual staff. Depending on your staff's tax status, you may be required to withhold income taxes based on your fiduciary responsibility, but not social security and Medicare taxes..

Employee

Under common-law rules, anyone who performs services for you is your employee *if you can control what will be done and how it will be done.* This is so, even when you give the employee freedom of action. What matters is that you have the right to control the details of how the services are performed. You will be required to withhold income tax and pay your employer portion of social security and Medicare matching the employee's withholdings and forward these amounts to the Internal Revenue Service. In addition an employee resource handbook will be helpful to let the employees understand what is expected of them. For each employee, your organization will be required to issue a Form W-2 at the end of the year, (normally December 31st) for earnings paid during that period. Your company will be required to file either a Form 941 or 945 and a corresponding Form 940 at year end as well. In addition to the federal requirements of matching social security and Medicare taxes, your respective state will require you to make payments into the unemployment compensation accounts for your employees as well.

When hiring either of the persons above, you will be required to adhere to labor and tax regulations. You will need to obtain from each person an application, a Form W-4 or W-9, an I-9, Medical criteria (depending upon your industry), licenses and certifications, credit reports and background checks. In addition, you should have an employee procedure or contract handbook for each person's review of your company's procedures and policies. These company policies should include information relative to performance evaluations, sick days, vacation, holidays, retirement information and exit interviews just to list a few.

S.Y.N.C. 7

Business Plan

Rule for Success

GET INVOLVED

Try to make the world a little better.
It's a great big world, overwhelming and
awe-inspiring. *What can I do*? You ask yourself.
Maybe you can't reform the world overnight,
but you can make your street, your school,
your church and/or your home a little better.
If everybody did that, it would be,
wouldn't it now,
a far better world for all of us.

Chapter 7

Business Plan

First, set up your budget of income and expenses for the first year. Remember, you are not going into business to borrow money but to make money. Therefore, any money you borrow will be used primarily to get the things you need to start or maintain your business.

The business plan can be as short as a statement of fact regarding your beginning a project, small business or hobby. Or it can be as detailed as to the total future of your life and/or business venture-- complete to the sale or dissolution of the occurrences.

Business Plans are Low Cost and Offer High Returns

Having a business plan is necessary for your survival in today's competitive business environment. A written business plan is as essential for a small business as it is for large corporations. A good business plan will help you focus on current and potential problems and assist you, your advisors, and employees in improving net profits.

Many owners of small businesses fail to put their plans in writing. It takes time to get your plan reduced to writing, and since there are so many other things to be done, the business plan goes unwritten. You wouldn't consider building a house without written plans to direct those who are assisting you. Likewise, you'll find your business more profitable if employees and advisors have a clear picture of what it is you are trying to accomplish.

The fact that you have reduced your business plan to writing does not mean that it's engraved in stone. Your business plan, like your building plan, is a guideline. Circumstances arise which will require that the plan be altered; that's as it should be.

Involve your employees in the development of the business plan. Your employees have a lot to offer and their involvement will make them more enthusiastic about putting the plan to work. At least once a year, you should hold a brainstorming session with your team, staff and family to review the following questions:

(1) Should we increase or decrease the line of products we offer?

(2) Is our marketing and advertising approach as effective as it can be?

(3) Are there employees whose work assignments should be redefined to make the company more efficient?

(4) What is the company's financial condition--past, present, and future? Are there policies which need to be changed to improve the financial condition?

(5) Where do we want the company to be a year from now, and five years from now?

Your business plan should be submitted along with your loan applications to convince your lenders that you are serious about your business and that you have the ability to repay borrowed money. A prospective investor will also be interested in your business plan. Large contracts may want a shorter version to assure you can provide the products or services they need to run their businesses in the future. In addition, you can use your business plan both as an operational guide as well as a tool to monitor the progress of your business as you grow.

Your business plan may also be used in obtaining grants for starting your small business, which are more desirable than a loan because grants don't have to be paid back. Unfortunately, federal grants for small business aren't readily available. However, there are ways to obtain small business start-up grants if you fit certain criteria. You may also be able to qualify for a specialized small business grants through many state agencies.

Why Your Small Business Should Have a Business Plan

If your company does not have a business plan, you are missing out on an excellent management tool. A written business plan outlines where the business is now, where you want it to be in the next three to five years, and what your strategy is for reaching those goals. The process of writing a plan will force you to think objectively about a range of issues.

During the process, you will work with key employees to solicit their views about the company and its goal. You will identify the challenges your company faces from its competition, changing demographics, or other outside forces. You will examine your current marketing approach and have an opportunity to realistically assess its effectiveness. You will spend time with your accountants, spotting trends in your financial picture before problems arise and forecasting future growth and cash flow needs. And, if you need additional capital or credit, having a business plan to give your banker is a great asset.

Your completed business plan might include the following:

- A statement about the business. Your product or service, your key employees, your main source of income, your competition, your suppliers and a description of your facilities and equipment.
- A summary of your marketing strategy. Your marketing activities and your competition's response to them, pricing and its effect on sales, the number, type, and anticipated growth of your customer base.
- Historical data. Past financial results, a review of how past goals were met or an explanation of why they were not met.
- Projections and forecasts. Financial and cash flow projections, coupled with specific plans for staffing, products and growth.

The following is an outline of items that should be included in your business plan narrative.

Suggested Outline of Business Plan

Review the outline below along with some of the other tasks you may have already completed. Use the following checklist to complete your business plan.

COVER SHEET: Name of business, names of principals, addresses and telephone number of business.

STATEMENT OF PURPOSE

TABLE OF CONTENTS

I. The Business

A. Description of business
B. Market
C. Competition
D. Location of business
E. Management
F. Personnel
G. Application and expected effect of loan (if needed)

II. Financial Data

A. Sources and applications of funding
B. Capital equipment list
C. Balance sheet
D. Breakeven analysis – (± See Page 70)
E. Income projections (Profit and Loss Statement)
    1. 3-year summary
    2. Detail by month for first year
    3. Detail by quarter for second and third years
    4. Notes of explanation
F. Projected Cash Flow
    1. Detail by month for first year
    2. Detail by quarter for second and third years
    3. Notes of explanation
G. Deviation analysis
H. Historical financial reports for existing business
    1. Balance sheets for past three years

2. Income statements for past three years
3. Tax returns

III. Supporting Documents

a. Personal resumes
b. Job descriptions
c. Personal financial statements
d. Credit reports
e. Letters of reference
f. Letters of intent
g. Copies of leases, contracts, legal documents
h. And anything else of relevance to the plan

SAMPLE FORMAT

BALANCE SHEET
Your Company
December 31, 20xx
(Unaudited)

| ASSETS | LIABILITIES AND NET WORTH |

Current Assets:

Cash $_____

Accounts Receivable_____

Merchandise Inventory_____

Supplies

Prepaid Expenses_____

Total: Current Assets $_____

Fixed Assets:

Fixtures & Leasehold
  Improvements **_____

Building _____

Equipment _____

Trucks/Vehicles _____
Less Accumulated
  Depreciation _____

Total: Fixed Assets $_____

Current Liabilities:

Accounts Payable_____

Current Portion of long-term
            Liabilities_____

Total: Current Liabilities_____

Long-Term Liabilities:

Notes Payable _____

Bank Loan Payable_____

Other Loans Payable_____

Total: Long-Term Liabilities
            $_____

Total Liabilities $_____

Net Worth:/Owner's Equity

_____

Total Assets $_____

Total Liabilities & Net Worth $_____

S.Y.N.C.

** If you have started a new business and have certain assets which will be transferred to your business, you should provide your accountant with the information listed on the "Checklist of Necessary Business Documents for Financial Statements" located in the reference materials section of this publication. These assets should be included in your business financial statements appropriately either at their cost or fair market value. The accountant should also discuss with you the depreciation methods available to you for a deduction on your financial statements and/or your income tax returns.

± -Breakeven analysis – This task is important to your actual cost of your product or service. The following is an example of components of a product's cost to determine a breakeven point for profits:

Cost of cake made from scratch includes the following information:

Direct cost = flour, milk, sugar, eggs, butter, flavoring, oil.

To compute this we need to know how may cakes we can make from 1 pound of flour, 1 gallon of milk, 1 pound of sugar, 1 dozen of eggs, 1 pound of butter, 6 ounces of flavor and 1 12 bottle of oil.

You will also need the cost, including tax if paid, of each ingredient above.

Indirect Cost = Location utilities, rent, insurance, repairs, appliances, utensils (cake pan, spoons, bowls & other measuring devices), mileage for grocery shopping, total time spent by the chef to prepare and decorate (this could be direct cost as well).

After gathering both the direct and indirect cost, you could compute the cost of each cake made and determine how many cakes you can make before you reach a breakeven point, then how many to make for your desired profit. You would also be able to calculate a profit margin and thusly attempt to improve upon our financial numbers overall.

SAMPLE FORMAT

Projected Income Statement
Your Company
January 1, 20xx - December 31, 20xx

GROSS Sales $_____

Less: COSTS OF GOODS SOLD   _____

GROSS Profit   _____

OPERATING EXPENSE:

    Salaries & Wages $_____

    Payroll Taxes & Benefits   _____

    Rent   _____

    Utilities   _____

    Maintenance   _____

    Advertising and Marketing Expense   _____

    Office Supplies   _____

    Postage   _____

    Automobile & Truck **   _____

    Insurance   _____

    Maintenance Delivery Equipment   _____

    Legal & Accounting   _____

    Depreciation   _____

    Transportation Expenses   _____

    Communications Expense   _____

    Research and Development Expenses   _____

OPERATING EXPENSE TOTAL $_____

OTHER EXPENSEs:

    Interest Payments   _____

OTHER TOTAL EXPENSE $_____

TOTAL EXPENSE $_____

PROFIT (LOSS) PRE-TAX   _____

TAXES Income Taxes (15% to 20%)   _____

TAXES -Social Security and Medicare (15.3%)   _____

S.Y.N.C.

Taxes - Corporate and LLC Franchise and
        Excise Taxes (10%) ***   _____

TOTAL TAXES   _____

NET PROFIT (LOSS) This represents your net pay from self-employment activities

_____

** Generally, the deduction of vehicles used in your business will be calculated
based on the amount of mileage used to perform your business activities. That's
why it is important you maintain a mileage log for related events in your
appointment book or scheduler. The actual method of computing your vehicle
expenses usually will not consistently be to your advantage as the vehicle(s) ages.

*** Sole Proprietorships do not pay a franchise and excise tax unless your
organizational structure is a single member LLC and has registered with your state's
Secretary of State Agency.

We recommend you refer to our

"Checklist of Necessary Business Documents
for Financial Statements and Income Tax
Preparation"

Located in the back of this publication and meet
with your Accountant to gather your materials
and complete this form.

SAMPLE FORMAT

PROJECTED CASH FLOW
Your Company
January 20XX

Beginning Cash Balance
Add Sales Revenue $_____

Other, including investments and funds borrowed   _____

Total Available Cash   _____

Deduct: Disbursements $_____
Cost of Materials   _____
Insurance   _____
Loan Payments   _____
Mortgage Payment   _____
Advertising   _____
Other operating expenses for which <u>money</u> was
       actually spent   _____

Deduct: Fixed Cash Disbursements

       Utilities $_____
       Salaries   _____
       Office Supplies   _____
       Telephone   _____
       Payroll Taxes   _____
Total Disbursements   _____

ENDING CASH BALANCE $_____

We do not recommend coding any expenses to the category of "Miscellaneous Expense" as this term does not have sufficient clarity.

We recommend you refer to our

"Checklist of Necessary Business Documents for Financial Statements and Income Tax Preparation"

Located in the back of this publication and meet with your Accountant to gather your materials and complete this form.

S.Y.N.C.

Chapter 8

Advertising and Promotion

Rule for Success

KEEP THE FAITH

You've heard it said often:
"Keep the faith, baby!"
You'll have reasons to lose faith in the course
of your life. Some people will betray your trust;
others will fail to keep promises.
But these breeches are no reason to turn sour
against the whole world.
Don't let that happen.
Retain your faith.
Believe in people.
Trust in God.
In other words, keep the faith.

Chapter 8

Advertising and Promotion

Marketing Plan

Your marketing plan should include all the information you have obtained in seeking out a viable plan for your company. In addition, it would be useful to compare your marketing ideas with the methods that are used by your competitors in this industry.

Comprehensive data about pricing strategies, specials to be offered to clients etc. should be included in this section. Details regarding your pricing and breakeven points will help you in targeting a more specific market to your product or service.

If you have designed a logo, your stationary and/or advertising materials, they should be included in your plan under "SUBSTANTIATION DOCUMENTATION". Remember that your branding will hopefully last throughout the life of your business and beyond. Some companies will revise logos and branding as their businesses begin to accelerate. Be sure to research color schemes and designs intently. Your branding should send a message to the consumer or buyer to *"Buy Me"*.

Modern technology gives us a variety of avenues to promote our product or services. Some of these media include Facebook, LinkedIn, Twitter, Blogs and other social network venues.

Some of the more conventional methods of marketing and advertising include the following:

Your Company's Stationary, Business Cards and Logo
Newspaper Advertising: – Local and Specifically Targeted
    Markets.
Magazine Advertising
Radio Advertising
Television Advertising
Cable Programming Advertising
Yellow Pages

Outdoor Advertising including Billboards
Direct Mailings
Email Ads
Specialty Advertising – Pens, Cups, Clothing, Magnets, Sticky
    Note Pads
Hand Bills and Flyers
Cold Calls with targeted emphasis
Customer Discount Programs
Major Chains Store Cash Register Tape Coupons
Social Media Campaigns

Start with a marketing budget and be sure to include the following basic items: business cards, website, logo design, stationary, packaging, product branding and newspaper advertising. In some cases a measurement of 2% to 5% of annual gross sales should be allocated to the marketing budget with various other factors taken into consideration. These percentages could be used in your business plan to determine your start-up cost budget as well.

Marketing Concept

Your marketing concept should include the importance of customers to a company and state the following information:

1. Determine the needs of your customers and who your customers are (Market Research)
2. Review and Analyze their competitive advantages within your specific industry (Market Strategy)
3. Select specific markets to serve based on your product or service (Target Marketing)
4. Determine how to satisfy those needs of your market (Market Mix).

Be sure to secure your own legal name as a domain name so when you become rich and famous someone else will not try to sell it back to you for an unreasonable price. Even if you do not intend to use it now it may be to your advantage to have down the road.

S.Y.N.C. 9

Organizational Structure of Proposed or Existing Business

Rule for Success

TRY YOUR HARDEST

Never do less than what you're capable of doing. You won't always succeed, but you'll know in your heart that you tried. Nothing is sadder than the terrible waste when a man/woman fails to live up to his/her potential, when he/she fail far short of achieving what everybody knows he/she could achieve. Try hard – it's a good feeling, and it's the only way to make the most of your God-given abilities.

Chapter 9

Organizational Structure of Proposed or Existing Business

Before you can decide how you want to structure your business, you'll need to know your options. The major concern regarding business structures is your understanding of how each organizational structure functions, what each means and the cost associated with each form of structure. Here's a brief rundown on the most common ways to organize a business.

- Sole Proprietorship
- Partnership
- Joint Venture
- Limited Partnership
- Limited Liability Company (LLC)
- Corporation (for-profit)
- Nonprofit Corporation (not-for-profit)
- Cooperative

For many new businesses, the best initial ownership structure is either a sole proprietorship or a partnership, if there is more than one owner/partner is involved. We recommend the sole proprietorship structure until the business has reached a certain threshold of gross income.

Sole Proprietorships

A sole proprietorship is a one-person business that is not registered, with the Secretary of State, like a limited liability company (LLC) or corporation. You don't have to do anything special or file any papers to set up a sole proprietorship. You create one just by going into business for yourself with a name, product or service and customers. Of course all businesses are required to file for a business license with the local and state tax authorities.

Legally, a sole proprietorship is inseparable from its owner--the business and the owner are one and the same. This means the owner of the business reports business income and losses on his or her personal tax return and is personally liable for any business-related obligations, such as debts or court judgments. Many people steer away from the structure based on being sued. To that, I ask the question, "Who would sue you and for what?" If you acquire unsecured debt, you will be responsible for paying it back. If you are providing products I would hope you performed your due diligence for certain research to avoid serious mistakes of this nature. Services oriented companies will normally purchase a liability policy for protection and errors of omission. Sole Proprietorship businesses file a Form 1040 – Schedule C with the Internal Revenue Service

Partnerships

Similarly, a partnership is simply a business owned by two or more people that haven't filed papers to become a corporation or a limited liability company (LLC). You don't have to file any paperwork to form a partnership--the arrangement begins as soon as you start a business with another person. As in a sole proprietorship, the partnership's owners pay taxes on their shares of the business income on their personal tax returns and they are each personally liable for the entire amount of any business debts and claims. This document should be filed with your local Registrars office as a notice of public record. Be sure to include language allowing each partner to exit should the need arises.

Sole proprietorships and partnerships make sense in a business where personal liability isn't a big worry, for example, a small service business in which you are unlikely to be sued and for which you won't be borrowing much money for inventory or other costs. Partnerships file a Form 1065 and issue a K-1 to each partner.

Joint Venture

A joint venture is where the business is managed by more than one person. A formal partnership may not necessarily be implemented at this point, as this structure will be more costly especially in direct relation to increases in accounting fees and tax liabilities to authorities. We recommend a written "Joint Venture" agreement detailing what is expected of each person financially and contractually as well. Basically, each person involved will agree to put certain funds, time or assets in to be used by the business venture.

A separate bank account would be opened which would require either two (2) persons or more to sign on transactions. The set of books implemented would keep track of all management and operating activity. At the end of the year these transactions would be split between each person and filed on their individual Schedule C to report their portion of the income or loss from the business activity. Once the group had interacted for a period of time either of the more complex structures could be implemented and funds should be available for the additional structure costs and expenses. We still recommend a written Joint Venture agreement for mutual terms and understandings. Accounting for a joint venture is performed in total during the operating period and separated at year end based on percentage of ownership. Each person involved will file their respective portion of activity on a Form 1040--Schedule C.

Limited Partnerships

Limited partnerships are costly and complicated to set up and run, and are not recommended for the average small business owner. Limited partnerships are usually created by one person or company (the "general partner"), who will solicit investments from others (the "limited partners").

The general partner controls the limited partnership's day-to-day operations and is personally liable for business debts (unless the general partner is a corporation or an LLC). Limited partners have minimal control over daily business decisions or operations and debts or claims. Consult a limited partnership expert if you're interested in creating this type of business. Partnerships file a Form 1065 and issue a K-1 to each partner.

Corporations and LLCs

Forming and operating an LLC or a corporation is a bit more complicated and costly, but well worth the trouble for some small businesses. The main benefit of an LLC or a corporation is that these structures limit the owners' personal liability for business debts and court judgments against the business.

What sets the corporation apart from all other types of businesses is that a corporation is an independent legal and tax entity, separate from the people who own, control and manage it. Because of this separate status, the owners of a corporation don't use their personal tax returns to pay tax on corporate profits--the corporation itself pays these taxes. Owners pay personal income tax only on money they draw from the corporation in the form of salaries, bonuses, and the like.

Like corporations, LLCs provide limited personal liability for business debts and claims. But when it comes to taxes, LLCs are more like partnerships: the owners of an LLC pay taxes on their shares of the business income on their personal tax returns.

Corporations and LLCs make sense for business owners who either (1) run a risk of being sued by customers or of piling up a lot of business debts, or (2) have substantial personal assets they want to protect from business creditors. C Corporations file a Form 1120 and usually pay the management a salary and issue a Form W-2. S-Corporations file a Form 1120-S and the shareholders receive a Form K-1 for operating activity to report on their Form 1040 at year end. Certain elections are required to become an S-Corporation.

Corporations should have regular board meetings to manage the affairs of the company. These should be written and documents in the board minutes.

Nonprofit Corporations

A nonprofit corporation is a corporation formed to carry out a charitable, educational, religious, literary, or scientific purpose. A nonprofit can raise much-needed funds by soliciting public and private grant money and donations from individuals and companies.

The federal and state governments do not generally tax nonprofit corporations on money they take in that is related to their nonprofit purpose, because of the benefits they contribute to society. Nonprofit corporations file a Form 990 with certain threshold limits.

Cooperatives

Some people dream of forming a business of true equals--an organization owned and operated democratically by its members.

These grassroots business organizers often refer to their businesses as a "group," "collective," or "co-op"; but these are often informal rather than legal labels. For example, a consumer co-op could be formed to run a food store, a bookstore, or any other retail business. Or a workers' co-op could be created to manufacture and sell arts and crafts. Most states do have specific laws dealing with the set-up of cooperatives, and in some states you can file paperwork with the secretary of state's office to have your cooperative formally recognized by the state. Check with your secretary of state's office for more information. Cooperatives file a Form 1120 - C.

Be sure to review the "Organizational Structure Summary" located in the back of this publication. All business tax forms will increase the cost of income tax preparation depending upon which type is chosen.

S.Y.N.C. 10

Accounting Systems and Bookkeeping Training

Rule for Success

SET GOALS FOR YOURSELF

Try to decide where you want to go, where you want to be in five years, ten years from now, and how you can get there. Change them whenever you need to along the way. You can't know now where you'll be half a lifetime from today, but you've got a far better chance if you plan and dream and work toward specific goals.

Chapter 10

Accounting Systems and Bookkeeping Training

Accounting and good record keeping is the foundation of the success of any business. Good recordkeeping means being organized, timely, knowledgeable and respectful of the operating activity of your business. There are many ways to maintain an accounting system for your business. Some are as follows:

1. Stand Alone Accounting Computer Double-Entry System
2. Internet Real Time Double Entry Accounting Systems
3. Spreadsheets (Single Entry System)
4. Manual Accounting Systems (Binder and Ledger Sheets)

There are a few basic Accounting terms every business person should be familiar with. There are only five (5) categories in which to code business activity. It is important to perform proper coding in books of record in order for your financial statements to reflect accurate information and help you to enhance your success.

1. Assets
2. Liabilities
3. Equity
4. Income
5. Expenses

Your record keeping should start with the *inception of your idea* to become self-employed because these early expenses and costs, if properly documented, may be used as business assets and expenses once the project is actually conceived. We strongly recommend you never code any transaction to "Miscellaneous" as this term has very little meaning and will misconstrue your financial information. The coding "Miscellaneous" may also increase scrutiny from tax authorities.

The following are more intricate details about accounting history and methods.

Single-entry Bookkeeping System
Versus
Double-entry Bookkeeping System

Single-entry Bookkeeping System

The single-entry bookkeeping system, also known as single-entry accounting system, is a method of bookkeeping relying on a one-sided accounting entry to maintain financial information.

Overview

Most businesses maintain a record of all transactions based on the double-entry bookkeeping system. However, many small, simple businesses maintain only a single-entry system that records the "bare essentials". In some cases only records of cash, accounts receivable, accounts payable and taxes paid may be maintained. Records of assets, inventory, expenses, revenues and other elements usually considered essential in an accounting system may not be maintained, except in memorandum form. Single-entry systems are usually inadequate except where operations are especially simple and the volume of operating activity is low.

A Bookkeeper or Accountant can typically compile this type of accounting system with additional information into an income statement and balance sheet. Maintaining a single-entry system normally will cost more in accounting fees to get to the end result due to the accountant having to pull information from several sources to obtain the financial reporting end result.

Advantages

Single-entry systems are used in the interest of simplicity. They are usually less expensive to be maintained by the self-employed person, than double-entry systems, because they do not require the services of a trained person.

Disadvantages

1. Data may not be available to management for effectively planning, overseeing and controlling the business.
2. Lack of systematic and precise bookkeeping may lead to inefficient administration and reduced control over the affairs of the business.
3. Single-entry records do not provide a check against clerical error, as does a double-entry system. This is one of the most serious defects of single-entry systems.
4. Single-entry records seldom make provision for recording all transactions. In addition, many internal transactions, such as adjusting entries are often not recorded.
5. Because no accounts are provided for many of the items appearing in both the Income Statement and Balance Sheet, omission of important data is possible.
6. In the absence of detailed records of all assets, lax administration of those assets may occur.
7. Theft and other losses are less likely to be detected.

Double-entry Bookkeeping System

The double-entry bookkeeping system was codified in the 15th century and refers to a set of rules for recording financial information in a financial accounting system in which every transaction or event changes at least two different accounts. In modern accounting this is done using debits and credits within the accounting equation: Equity = Assets - Liabilities. The accounting equation serves as a kind of error-detection system. If at any point the sum of debits does not equal the corresponding sum of credits, an error has occurred.

Since several different types of errors result in equal sums for debits and credits, double-entry accounting is not a guarantee that no errors have been made. Many of the common errors are in the actual coding of transactions to an improper chart of account.

Timeline

Century	Development Stage
12th	There are traces of the double-entry system in the accounting of the Islamic world from at least the 12th century.
13th	The earliest extant records that follow the modern double-entry form are those of Amatino Manucci, a Florentine merchant at the end of the 13th century.
14th	Some sources suggest that Giovanni di Bicci de' Medici introduced this method for the Medici bank in the 14th century.
15th	By the end of the 15th century, the merchant ventures of Venice used this system widely. Fra Luca Pacioli, a monk and collaborator of Leonardo da Vinci, first codified the system in a mathematics textbook of 1494. Pacioli is often called the "father of accounting" because he was the first to publish a detailed description of the double-entry system, thus enabling others to study and use it. His "textbook" of accounting with very little modification would be used for the next 500 years.
	The present day trial balance sheet did not get its form until 1868 and the income statement or profit and loss was developed before WWII. In the 1980s, Statements of Financial Position were developed with the purpose to provide relevant "information about the operating, financing, and investing activities of an enterprise and the effects of those activities on cash resources".

Accounts

An accounting system records, retains and reproduces financial information relating to financial transaction flows and financial position. Financial Transaction Flows encompass primarily inflows on account of investment and incomes and outflows on account of expenses and withdrawals. Elements of financial position, including property, money received, or money spent, are assigned to one of the primary groups i.e. Assets, liabilities, and equity.

Within these primary groups each distinctive asset, liability, income and expense is represented by its respective "account". An account is simply a record of financial inflows and outflows in relation to the respective asset, liability, equity, income or expense. Income and expense accounts are considered temporary accounts, since they represent only the inflows and outflows absorbed in the financial-position elements on completion of the time period, normally twelve (12) months.

Account types (nature)

Type	Represent	Examples
Real	Physically tangible things in the real world and certain intangible things not having any physical existence	Tangibles - Plant and Machinery, Furniture and Fixtures, Computers and Information Processing Equipment etc. Intangibles - Goodwill, Patents and Copyrights
Personal	Business and Legal Entities	Individuals, Partnership Firms, Corporate entities, Non-Profit Organizations, any local or statutory bodies including governments at country, state or local levels
Nominal	Income and Expenditure Accounts for recognition of the implications of the financial transactions during each fiscal year until finalization of accounts at the end	Sales, Purchases, Electricity Charges

Example: A sales account is opened for recording the sales of goods or services and at the end of the financial period the total sales are transferred to the revenue statement account (Profit and Loss Account or Income and Expenditure Account).

Similarly, expenses during the financial period are recorded using the respective Expense accounts, which are also transferred to the revenue statement account. The net positive or negative balance (profit or loss) of the revenue statement account is transferred to reserves or capital account as the case may be.

Account types (periodicity of flow)

The classification of accounts into real, personal and nominal is based on their nature, i.e. physical assets, liability or financial transactions.

The further classification of accounts is based on the periodicity of their inflows or outflows in the context of the fiscal year.

Income is immediate inflow during the fiscal year. Expense is the immediate outflow during the fiscal year.

An asset is a long-term inflow with implications extending beyond the financial period, and by the traditional view could represent unclaimed income. Alternatively, an asset could be valued at the present value of its future inflows.

Liability is long-term outflow with implications extending beyond the financial period, and by the traditional view could represent unamortized expense. Alternatively, a liability could be valued at the present value of future outflows.

Type of accounts	Long term inflows	Long term outflows	Short term inflows	Short term outflows
Real accounts	Assets			
Personal accounts	Assets	Liability		
Nominal accounts			Incomes	Expenses

Items in accounts are classified into five broad groups, also known as the elements of the accounts: Asset, Liability, Equity, Revenue and Expense.

The classification of Equity as a distinctive element for classification of accounts is disputable on account of the "Entity concept", since for the objective analysis of the financial results of any entity the external liabilities of the entity should not be distinguished from any contribution by the shareholders.

Accounting Entries

- The double-entry accounting system records financial transactions in relation to asset, liability, equity, income or expense related to it through accounting entries.
- Any accounting entry in the double-entry accounting system has two effects: one of increasing one account as a debit/credit, the other of decreasing another account by an equal amount as a debit/credit.
- If the accounting entries are recorded without error, at any point in time the aggregate balance of all accounts having positive balances will be equal to the aggregate balance of all accounts having negative balances.
- The double-entry bookkeeping system ensures that the financial transaction has equal and opposite effects in two different accounts.
- Accounting entries use terms such as debit and credit to avoid confusion regarding the opposite effect of the accounting entry. For example, if an accounting entry debits a particular account, the opposite account will be credited and vice versa.
- The rules for formulating accounting entries are known as "Golden Rules of Accounting".
- The accounting entries are recorded in the "Books of Accounts".

Books of Accounts

It does this by ensuring that each individual financial transaction is recorded in at least two different nominal ledger accounts within the financial accounting system. (Nominal accounts in accounting are considered temporary accounts.) The two entries have equal amounts and opposite signs, so that when all entries in the accounts are summed, the total is exactly the same: and the accounts balance. This is a partial check that each and every transaction has been correctly recorded. The transaction is recorded as a "debit record"

(Dr.) in one account, and a "credit record" (Cr) entry in the other account. The debit entry will be recorded on the debit side (left-hand side) of a nominal ledger account and the credit entry will be recorded on the credit side (right-hand side) of a nominal ledger account. A nominal ledger has a Debit (left) side and a Credit (right) side. If the total of the entries on the debit side is greater than the total on the credit side of the nominal ledger account, that account is said to have a debit balance. Banking Debits and Credits are opposite of accounting Debits and Credits.

An example of an entry being recorded twice for double-entry bookkeeping, using the accrual method of accounting, would be a supplier's invoice for stationery costing $100. The expense or Debit entry is Stationery Expense (Nominal Ledger expense account) $100 Dr. (showing that $100 has been spent on stationery) and the Credit entry is to the Supplier's Accounts Payable Control (Nominal Ledger accounts payable) $100 Cr (showing that we now owe the supplier $100). This transaction has now been recorded twice in the financial accounting system and the total value is $100 for both Debit and Credit values.

Double entry is used only in nominal ledgers. It is not used in daybooks, which normally do not form part of the nominal ledger system. The information from the daybooks will be used in the nominal ledger but it is the nominal ledgers that will ensure the integrity of the resulting financial information created from the daybooks (provided that the information recorded in the daybooks is correct).

(The reason for this is to limit the number of entries in the nominal ledger: entries in the daybooks can be totaled before they are entered in the nominal ledger. If there are only a relatively small number of transactions it may be simpler instead to treat the daybooks as an integral part of the nominal ledger and thus of the double-entry system.)

However, as can be seen from the examples of daybooks shown below, it is still necessary to check, within each daybook, that the postings from the daybook balance.

The double entry system uses nominal ledger accounts. From these nominal ledger accounts a Trial balance can be created. The trial balance lists all the nominal ledger account balances. The list is split into two columns, with debit balances placed in the left hand column and credit balances placed in the right hand column. Another column will contain the name of the nominal ledger account describing what each value is for. The total of the debit column must equal the total of the credit column.

From the Trial balance the Profit and Loss Statement and the Balance Sheet can then be produced. The Profit and Loss statement will contain nominal ledger accounts that are Income or Expense type nominal ledger accounts. The Balance Sheet will contain ledger accounts that consist of Asset or Liability and Equity accounts.

Bookkeeping Process

The bookkeeping process refers primarily to recording the financial effects of transactions into accounts and categories. The variation between manual and any electronic accounting system stems from the latency between the recording of the financial transaction and it's posting in the relevant account. This delay, absent in electronic accounting systems due to instantaneous posting into relevant accounts, is not replicated in manual systems, thus giving rise to primary books of accounts such as Sales Journal, Receipts Journal, Disbursement Journal and Purchase Journal for recording the immediate effect of the financial transaction.

In the normal course of business, a document is produced each time a transaction occurs. Sales and purchases usually have invoices or receipts. Deposit slips are produced when deposits are made to a bank account. Checks are written to pay money out of the account. Bookkeeping involves, first of all, recording the details of all of these source documents into multi-column journals or Excel spreadsheets (also known as a set of books of first entry or daysheets). For example, all sales are recorded in the Sales Journal and all Check Payments are recorded in the Check Disbursement Journal. Each column in a journal normally corresponds to an account. In the single entry system, each transaction is recorded only once. Most

93

individuals who balance their checkbooks each month are using such a system, and most personal finance software follows this approach.

After a certain period, typically a month, the columns in each journal are each totaled to give a summary for the period. Using the rules of double entry, these journal summaries are then transferred to their respective accounts in the ledger, or book of accounts, whether manual or computer accounting software. For example the entries in the Sales Journal are taken and a debit entry is made in each customer's account (showing that the customer now owes us money) and a credit entry might be made in the account for "Income - Sale of Class 2 Widgets" (showing that this activity has generated revenue for us). This process of transferring summaries or individual transactions to the ledger is called posting. Once the posting process is complete, accounts kept using the "T" format undergo balancing, which is simply a process to arrive at the balance of the account.

As a partial check that the posting process was done correctly, a working document called an unadjusted trial balance is created. In its simplest form, this is a three-column list. The first column contains the names of each chart of accounts number and name in the ledger, which have a non-zero balance. If an account has a debit balance, the balance amount is copied into column two (the debit column). If an account has a credit balance, the amount is copied into column three (the credit column). The debit column is then totaled and then the credit column is totaled. The two totals must agree - this agreement is not by chance - because under the double-entry rules, whenever there is a posting, the debits of the posting equal the credits of the posting. If the two totals do not agree, an error has been made either in the journals or during the posting process. The error must be located and rectified and the totals of debit column and credit column recalculated to check for agreement before any further processing can take place.

Once the accounts balance, the accountant makes a number of adjustments and changes the balance amounts of some of the accounts. These adjustments must still obey the double-entry rule. For example, the "Inventory" asset account might be changed to bring it in line with the actual numbers counted during an actual inventory count. At the same time, the expense account associated with usage of inventory is adjusted by an equal and opposite amount. Other adjustments such as posting mileage, depreciation and prepayments are also done at this time. These journal entries result in an account listing referred to as an adjusted trial balance. It is the accounts in this list and their corresponding debit or credit balances that are used to prepare the financial statements.

Finally, financial statements are drawn from the trial balance, which may include:

- The Income Statement, also known as the Statement of Financial Results, Profit and Loss Statement, or P & L.
- The Balance Sheet, also known as the Statement of Financial Position.
- The Cash Flow Statement.
- The Statement of Retained Earnings, also known as the Statement of Total Recognized Gains and Losses or Statement of Changes in Equity.
- The Statement of Changes in Financial Position.

Computer Accounting Systems

There are many computerized accounting systems available. However, many small business owners are not familiar enough with accounting methods and processes to correctly implement these box systems accurately. We strongly encourage each of you to interview your accountant, as we have recommended in the team section of this publication, to be assured you can and will grow in this area as well. It is critical for an owner to be able to read and comprehend the business financial statements in direct correlation to the business activities taking place in the company. The best accounting system is one which allows both your office and the accountant's office to perform task in "Real-Time" to your books of record.

We strongly encourage your books of record to be implemented with a numerical chart of accounts system. This will further assure your data is posted into the proper categories and should promote a cleaner financial statement presentation.

If your accounting system is set up correctly, it should be maintained with ease. If you have questions or need assistance, please call us at 615.333.3330. We, as always, are excited to share our profession with our readers and clients. Please make notes or highlight any areas you may need us to explain or assist you with implementation. We will review your business and attempt to make appropriate recommendations. Therefore, it is important that your system is implemented correctly from Day 1.

Be sure to review the "Checklist of Necessary Business Documents for Financial Statements and Income Tax Preparation" in the back of this publication.

S.Y.N.C. 11

Business Banking Process Information

Rule for Success

LOOK UP TO SOMEBODY

Identify with somebody. Don't be embarrassed to have a hero or two. Pattern your life – parts of your life– after somebody you admire. Don't ever be reluctant to believe in somebody and to learn from their trials and triumphs.

Chapter 11

Business Banking Process Information

Business Bank Account Setup and Use

Open a checking account with a friendly personable Loan Officer to establish a sound long-term business banking relationship.

- Be confident, enthusiastic and well prepared.
- Determine if you need a small bank or large bank for your goals and banking needs.
- Branch offices are also important to determine accessibility.

Checking Account Criteria

Request your bank to provide you with a hardcopy statement for your monthly activity. Be sure to request, if this is not a criterion, cut-off activity at the end or near the end of each month (e.g., 29-31 day of the month). Also request the larger four (4) on a page copies of all cancelled checks which normally show the front and back of each check. If, however, you are performing financial tasks via the internet, simply download your bank information monthly in the following two formats.

Request from the bank or order from a check printing service a three (3) ring checkbook binder with three check stubs per page or you may purchase a One-Write Check Writing System. Even if you plan to write checks on your computer, there are always times you need to write checks out of the office.

Research the need for an interest bearing checking account which may require a minimum account balance to be maintained either in this account or another account housed at the same bank.

On a monthly basis the following accounting or bookkeeping function should be performed.

1. Download your bank statements and all supporting documents in Portable Document Format (**PDF**)
2. Download your detail transactions in comma-separated values (**CSV**) or as an Excel format (XLS or XLSX)

This process should be done for all bank accounts, credit cards, PayPal, eBay, mortgage and credit union transactions. Some institutions will store your data for as much as twenty-four months, others only six months. Be sure to check with your financial institutions and know each one's policy.

If you plan to primarily use your debit/credit card, remember the notes the accountant would like for you to make in the memo section of each check regarding purchases. This will need to be done on each individual receipt you obtain for those electronic transactions.

When issuing a check always complete the check stub first and show all information relative to the transaction. For example, Invoice # or PO #. If utilities, property location and account number. If communications, the related phone number. If loan payment or credit card, loan number or credit card account number. After completing the checkbook stub information, be sure to write on the invoice or bill from the vendor the following information:

1. Date Paid
2. Check Number (#)
3. Amount Paid ($)
4. Person processing

See our "sample completed check stub and check" in the back of the publication on page 158.

Always use checks in their pre-numbered sequence. We recommend beginning with either a 4 digit or 3 digit check #, for example 1372. Vendors sometimes question a new business with small check numbers. The larger numbers reflect "being in business for a while". In addition, when you use your check in sequence you are more quickly determine if some have become missing.

Deposit Book Criteria:

Always label the cover of your Deposit Books with the first date of use and the last date of use or label them in numerical sequence starting with the # 1 and the year XXXX. (April 15, 20XX to July 31, 20XX).

The standard term "Duplicate Deposit Book" usually refers to a deposit book with both white and yellow slips which are usually carbonless. However, this type is more expensive than all white deposit slips which will work just fine. The all white deposit slips usually have a couple sheets of carbon paper in the back of each book.

When using all white duplicates, be sure to insert a piece of carbon paper between the two slips so you can maintain a copy in your book. The white or top slip is maintained in your deposit book and the bottom, carbon copy, is given to the bank to be processed with the items you are depositing.

Be sure to include the following information on each deposit slip and follow the subsequent processing procedure:

a. Name of person you are receiving funds from.
b. Purpose of funds being received, if not from regular customer sales
c. If a check is written in another company or person's name, list that information as well.
d. Include the check number, money order number or receipt number for the item you are depositing.
e. Any check stubs or receipts received from the client should be stapled to the back of the deposit ticket to remain in the deposit book as supporting documentation.
f. After making the deposit at the bank, the receipt the bank issues to you should be stapled to the back of the duplicate deposit slip left in the deposit book.

See the completed "Copy of Completed Deposit Slip and Instructions" and a "Copy of Completed Check and Check Stub with Instructions" in the back of this publication.

Receipt Book for Cash Transactions

A Receipt Book should be used for cash transactions coming into the business and cash expenses paid from the business matters.

Preferred type of Receipts Book to purchase:

The Receipt Book should at least three (3) colored copies, four (4) receipts per page and be imprinted with pre-numbered sequence receipt numbers.

The three copies should be considered as follows:

1. White - Goes to Client/Customer or Vendor
2. Yellow - To be attached to duplicate deposit slip in deposit book noted above
3. Blue - Remains in the Receipt Book for future reference and accounting processing.

See the completed "Copy of Completed Deposit Slip and Instructions" and a "Copy of Completed Check and Check Stub with Instructions" in the back of this publication.

S.Y.N.C. 12

Receipts and Financial Transactions

Rule for Success

BE KIND

Kindness costs nothing, and yet it can mean so much. A kind word, a kind gesture, any small act of kindness may be remembered forever – and you'll know inside you that it was the right thing to do.

Chapter 12

Receipts and Financial Transactions

Remember, your original transactions set the wheels in motion for a solid accounting and financial system. When your original transactions are well labeled and appropriately reflect what you have done, it will be less costly to set up your accounting system and more assurance your financial statements are correct coded and accurate.

Receipts are valuable to your business in a number of ways.

- Receipts document how you have made certain transactions in doing business in the past
- Receipts document your expenses and allow certain items to be used in the preparation of your income tax returns, which reduces your income tax liability.
- Receipts will be helpful in the planning of your business's future. You may want to repeat an action which was successful or decide not to repeat an action that may have cost you money.

Either way, receipts are your original documentation and ultimately become the backbone of your business.

Be sure to fold each of your receipts with the printed side inside itself. The receipts you receive from most vendors will fade away in a matter of time. You may want to write the information in ink to preserve the information for later use. We then recommend you place the receipt in a large plastic zip lock bag until you return to the office or your desk to hand them off for further future processing.

Some people prefer to do business in cash, not necessarily because they do not have choices but because they have a certain comfort level in dealing in cash. This method of handling transactions becomes more tedious and challenging to maintain long term and much more costly to account for due to the volume of actual transaction receipts to process.

When you process multiple transactions in cash, you must obtain and maintain a receipt for each transaction, because there is no other way to know how your business was conducted. When you spend cash and do not retain receipts, think of a bird, flying through the sky with your money in their beaks and once that bird is out of site, so is your money and business deductions.

When you make your purchases either with a debit or credit card, you should retain your receipts and attach them to the appropriate bank statement or credit card statement to be submitted to your accountant monthly, quarterly or annually with your paperwork for processing. As an alternative, review the receipt process noted below. Remember to fold each receipt with the print to the inside.

Receipt Processing:

Once you have all of your receipts in one place, you or your staff need to organize them for entry into the accounting system. The following method of processing receipts should be performed for all actual paper receipts:

1. First make notes on each receipt in ink including the date, vendor (abbreviated for speed), dollar amount and purpose. Over time some receipts will fade and the ink will disappear.
2. Separate all receipts between cash, debit and credit card receipts.
3. Gather a few envelopes, or use the ones you throw away for the bills that come in, or a regular # 10, label with the months of the year, January through December, XXXX.
4. Insert your debit receipts into their envelopes
5. Insert your credit card receipts into their envelopes
6. We recommend you perform this task on a monthly basis; therefore, your receipts will be organized at the end of the year.
7. Cash receipts will need to be processed further as follows:
    a. After labeling each receipt, sort each receipt into categories for example food, office supplies, ingredients, gasoline, product cost, communications expenses, money order fees, employee lunches, uniforms etc.
    b. Once sorted run an adding machine tape on each category by month.
    c. Submit to your accountant or bookkeeper so this information can be included in your business books of record as expenses for the period.

The preferred method of doing business transactions is to use a debit card or credit card. It reduces the work involved in attempting to keep up with expenses and documenting transactions in your business.

The more details you can keep track of and give, the better your accountant can serve you. Make notes on the actual receipts, in your scheduler or with a voice memo. Include the date of the event, with whom you met, the nature of the meeting, results, cost and place of the meeting or event.

Success in business requires a sound cash management program. Your goal should be to get your cash working for you as fast as possible; keep it working as long as possible and maximize the benefit while it's working.

To get cash working for you faster, speed up your billing procedures. Try to invoice on the day you ship or soon after, and deposit checks the day you receive them. Consider offering discounts for fast payment and loyal clients. Monitor accounts receivable and follow up on slow payers. If a customer is late paying his bill, call and find out why. Consider charging interest on delinquent accounts. Be sure to research the maximum rates allowed in your state. The state of Tennessee max is 14.00%.

Balance the benefit of holding onto your money as long as possible with two other considerations:

1) Discounts for paying your bills promptly
2) Good will with your suppliers.

If no discount is offered, pay on the last day possible. For large purchases, consider negotiating a longer pay period or a graduated one. Never pay sales tax to a supplier until you have confirmed that it is required.

Monitor inventory closely and avoid tying up cash unnecessarily. Have employees use credit cards to pay for travel and entertainment. It is a good idea for them to submit actual receipts with details of each along with their travel logs.

To quickly identify available cash, and to save time reconciling statements, concentrate your cash in one bank account. Then set up an accurate cash forecasting system. Know ahead of time when cash will arrive and when it will be needed for disbursements. This will allow you to invest extra cash wisely to increase interest earnings, or to identify shortages early, thus decreasing interest expense. Never leave large amounts in non-interest bearing accounts for any period of time.

Vehicle Mileage or Actual Expenses

Mileage is an excellent way to reduce your taxable income without spending additional dollars. It is important to maintain records of actual odometer readings from each vehicle used for both business and personal. When recording this expense in your books of record, we use the following calculation:

Total miles driven for the year
        Divided by
Allocated business mileage
        Equals
Percentage of use for business.

Example: Total miles driven this year =   15,000 miles/
Business miles used to perform business tasks   9233 miles =

Percentage of business use   61.55 %

The deduction would be as follows:
9233 miles x 56.5 ¢   = $ 5,216.65
Plus Interest Expense 1,725.36 x 61.55% =   1,061.95
Total Vehicle Mileage Rate Deduction = $ 6,278.60

The usage of the mileage rate includes the following actual vehicle expenses when calculating your mileage deduction:

1. Cost of fuel and oil
2. Repairs and maintenance, including parts and labor
3. Insurance
4. Motor vehicle tags and registration
5. Depreciation of original cost

In addition to the mileage rate, the following expenses are also considered a business deduction:

1. Interest expense
2. Parking and tolls

We have included the mileage rates, reflecting the past several years, to assist you with computing your reimbursement or deduction of this expense once you have actually decided to start your business. In addition to mileage rate calculation, you are also able to take a deduction for any interest you paid on your vehicle(s) calculated based on your percentage of use for your business activity.

Individuals who are employees will use the above method to report "Employee Business Expenses" as a Miscellaneous Deduction on their income tax returns.

See our "Automobile/Vehicle Expense Worksheet" and "Internal Revenue Service Mileage Rates" in our Reference Materials and Checklist section of this publication.

Entertainment and Meals

Entertainment and meals which are a business related may be a deduction when you meet with customers, employees or when entertaining a client. Certain requirements need to be met in order to legitimate the expenses. In most cases you will get a deduction of 50% of the expense, but you will need to provide your accountant with the total amounts spent.

You can deduct entertainment expenses only if they are both ordinary and necessary and meet one of the following tests:

- Directly-related test.

To meet the directly-related test for entertainment expenses (including entertainment-related meals), you must show that:

1. The main purpose of the combined business and entertainment was the active conduct of business,

2. You did engage in business with the person during the entertainment period, and
3. You had more than a general expectation of getting income or some other specific business benefit at some future time.

- Associated test.

Even if your expenses do not meet the directly-related test, they may meet the associated test.

To meet the associated test for entertainment expenses (including entertainment-related meals), you must show that the entertainment is:

1. Associated with the active conduct of your trade or business, and
2. Directly before or after a substantial business discussion

Be sure to review Chapter 17 – Getting Organized and What to Keep.

S.Y.N.C. 13

Business Licensing, Permits, Credentials and Inspections

Rule for Success

GET AN EDUCATION

Do everything that's required –
whatever you must do – to get an
education. Go as far as you can go in
school. Don't drop out, despite all
the temptations. The benefits of that
education will be with you all your
life – and it will help you in so many
ways to get where you want to go and
achieve the goals you want to
achieve.

Chapter 13

Business Licensing, Permits, Credentials and Inspections

Many states and local governments require you to register with their organization when you start a new business venture. Once you have registered, you may be required to report income, assets and other financial information of which you will be required to pay an annual tax to those local agencies. All states have websites which can be easily accessed via the internet to research the requirements for your business activity.

In most cases your business tax licenses will be due annually depending upon your class of business activity. Personality taxes may be due on certain non real estate equipment, furniture and vehicles used in your business. These taxes may be used as a deduction on your business tax licenses as well.

As the business owner, you should research sales tax regulations regarding your products and services. If you are required to collect sales tax, you would need to apply for a Sales Tax Number. (This is not your Employer Identification Number.) This number will allow you to purchase your Cost of Goods Sold without paying sales tax based on being used in the creation of your product to be resold. There are many variations in the calculation of sales tax depending upon type, dollar amount of items and location of sales. You may be required to report and pay your sales taxes monthly, quarterly or annually. Many states have a threshold which may require your company to electronically file the reports via the internet. Sales tax rules vary from state to state. We strongly encourage you to take one of the free sales tax classes to be sure you understand how to compute sales tax to be collected on your products or services. The variations are numerous when reviewing detailed sales tax rule calculations. For example, some agencies charge a different rate on items sold at a price in excess of $2,500.00. In other jurisdictions food is taxed at a lower or no sales tax rate. Sales tax is a pass through liability from your customers and paid directly by you to the tax authority. You collect the sales tax from the customer and then forward the same amount on to the taxing authorities. This process becomes costly when the forms are not completed correctly or in a timely manner. Then, this practice is costing your business money.

Many industries will require you to have been an apprentice, working for someone in the industry, before you can receive your own self sufficient credentials.

Be sure to authenticate your credentials with all regulatory boards and governmental agencies that require you to do so, as fines later could be steep.

When searching for a physical location you may determine that you will need to perform a few improvements to the space to be leased. Before you sign your lease agreement, check with the local code, fire and permit departments to determine if the location is a good fit for your business operation and that it meets all the authority's specifications as well. These departments will be able to inform you if a permit or special license is required for your business to operate in the space. It would be very difficult if you signed the lease and the code department explained the location could not have a commercial oven in it for you to make your cupcakes. I am sure the landlord will still want their rent.

Many professional industries which provide services require the individuals to complete certain standardized examinations or maintain a certain level of credentials. They are also required to maintain a level of continuing education over a designated period of time and pay annual fees to operate in a particular area. Some professions have oversight committees and registration boards which include the following:

Accountancy
Alarm Systems Contractors Board
Architectural & Engineering Examiners
Auctioneer Commission
Barber Examiners
Collection Service
Contractors/Home Improvement
Cosmetology
Funeral Directors, Embalmers and Burial Services
Geology

Health Care Professionals
Home Inspector Licensing Advisory
Land Surveyors
Limited Licensed Electricians
Limited Licensed Plumbers
Locksmith Licensing Program Advisory
Mortgage and Finance Brokers
Motor Vehicle Commission
Pre-Trial Mediators
Private Investigation & Polygraph Commission
Private Probation Service Council
Private Protective Services
Race Track Licensing Program
Real Estate Appraisers
Real Estate Commission
Scrap Metals Registration Program
Soil Scientist Licensing Program

Be sure you know your
licensing requirements
before you hang out a
shingle.

Education is meant to train you in your chosen field of interest. When you are engaged in your chosen career, you are performing task directly related to your passion. If you find yourself working in a career which does not provide a level of happiness and rewards, maybe it is time to retool yourself and think of what your options would be.

S.Y.N.C. 14

Business Location

Rule for Success

NEVER GIVE UP

You'll encounter setbacks along the way, setbacks that seem ruinous and even final. They'll depress you, crush your spirit. But you must refuse to accept defeat. Make sure your setbacks are only temporary. Fight back. Learn to defy hard luck. Learn from adversity. Never stop trying, for there's always another way, usually a better way. Take heart from the knowledge that many of the world's most renowned leaders throughout history overcame immense obstacles, rebounded from crushing defeat, and refused stubbornly to yield to seeming disaster.

Chapter 14

Business Location

Home Office

You may be able to deduct a portion of the costs of your home if you operate a full or part-time business there. The tax write-off could include a share of utilities, insurance, repairs, property taxes, mortgage interest, and depreciation (or rent, if you don't own your home). There should be no fear of reasonable home office expenses as long as this is where you and staff work, meet clients and manage the affairs of your business.

Your home office must be used exclusively and regularly as your principal place of business or as a place to meet clients or customers and where your staff works. To prove you use your home office regularly, you should work there more than a few hours a month. Until recently, your home office had to be the focal point of your business, where the bulk of your business revenue was earned. However, if you meet or deal with patients, clients, or customers in your home in the normal course of your business, even though you also carry on business at another location, you can deduct your expenses for the part of your home used exclusively and regularly for business if you meet both the following tests

- You physically meet with patients, clients, customers or staff on your premises.
- Their use of your home is substantial and integral to the conduct of your business.

You get no deduction for performing your employer's work in your home unless you are required by your employer to do so. You cannot deduct space you use merely to manage your investments or rental property. Some investors and real estate owners can opt to be considered as self-employed and file their income and expenses on a Form Schedule C. These investors are considered as "Traders" and real estate owners as "Real Estate Professional". In order to be considered as a self-employed business, work should be performed on a full-time at least forty (40) hour basis and the related activities should be performed regularly and consistently. When this tax election is chosen, those individuals will pay income tax on their earnings as well as social security and Medicare tax which is 15.3% on the net income shown on the Schedule C.

The space you claim for a write-off can be a room or part of a room that is partitioned off for business use. Measure the portion of your home used for your business, then divide by your total square feet of your home to obtain a percentage of use factor. This factor will be used to calculate your actual home office business deduction and thereby allowing you to deduct that share of your total home office expenses. You can't write off more expense than you have business income, however, you still need to perform the calculation so these expenses can be rolled over to the next year or to a year in which your business activity reflects a net profit.

Beginning in tax year 2013 (returns filed in 2014), taxpayers may use a simplified option when figuring the deduction for business use of their home. This simplified option does not change the criteria for who may claim a home office deduction. It merely simplifies the calculation and recordkeeping requirements of the allowable deduction. It is wise to compare the simplified option with the regular option to determine the best deduction.

Be sure to meet with your accountant so you can be sure of the calculation, the items you can include as home office expenses and understand what you need to keep up with both short-term and long-term. Home office should not be feared as long as you are educated regarding the process.

Purchased Office Space

We do not recommend purchasing a commercial building unless you are a seasoned small business owner with a very positive financial track record. When you decide you are ready to purchase a commercial office location, make sure your business plan and projected budget will support your decision.

Rental or Leasing of Office Space

For many people, leasing business real estate makes good financial sense. Often leasing means a smaller cash outlay and more flexibility than buying. If you are considering leasing, evaluate the following factors:

Location

For most businesses, the location for customer access can either make or break you. Will the building meet your current and future space requirements? Does the location have enough parking for your customers, employees and delivery vehicles?

If there are other tenants on the premises, are their business operations compatible with yours? Also check the landlord's track record concerning repairs and maintenance.

Is the property currently zoned for your business requirements, and are there any pending zoning changes which will affect the desirability of the location?

Cost

The cost of a lease is usually broken down into the cost per square foot. To determine the true cost, you should understand the difference between rental (total) space and usable (revenue-producing) space. You should also be familiar with the terms "gross" and "net". Under a gross lease, the landlord pays for insurance, property taxes, utilities and maintenance. Under a net lease, you pay.

If alterations have to be made to the property, agree in writing who is paying, how much and for what. You would need to contact local authorities for inspections, permits and code to determine if this location is suitable for the type of business you plan to operate. This needs to be done before you sign the lease agreement. We recommend you possibly place a small deposit with the landlord to hold the property until you are able to successfully complete your compliance of the location as related to your business.

Options

Various options can be included in the lease to ensure flexibility. The usual options cover renewal, subleasing and eventual purchase by the tenant and cancellation by either party.

A lease is a binding legal agreement. Your attorney should draft or review the document before you commit to any terms. Avoid long-term commitments. Rent space on a month-to-month basis until you know that you have need for a long-term lease. Determine that the space will fulfill your needs for the lease term.

Business Centers

Business incubator centers offer programs that nurture the successful development of entrepreneurial companies through an array of business support resources and services. Business accelerators, similar to incubators, provide services; however, on a compressed timeline assisting you with bringing products and services to market in matter months.

There are many business centers which will allow you to rent their space on an "as needed basis". Of course prior scheduling and arrangements will be required along with a small monthly or annual fee. Normally these locations will provide you with a meeting or conference room, projector equipment, computers, copying and faxing services, communication equipment for conference calls and monitors for attendees located in other places. The advantage to using a ready-made office is low cost, accessibility, comfort of attendees, scheduling and ease of use for you to operate effectively. Investigate several options to determine which will better suit your needs.

Home Office

S.Y.N.C. 15

Getting Hard Copies Organized and What to Keep

Rule for Success

SUCCESS

Success is not something to wait for,
but it is something to work for

Chapter 15

Getting Hard Copies Organized and What to Keep

When was the last time you couldn't find an important paper you knew you had carefully put away someplace? How much time do you spend trying to straighten out your business and personal affairs, especially at income tax time?

How, in fact, do people decide what records are important to keep and what they can discard? How do they decide where to store and keep these records and papers?

Even though each family or household must work out its own system, some general guidelines can be helpful. As a starter, ask yourself a few questions:

• How easy or difficult would it be for other members of your household to figure out your record system? Or...do you even have a system?

• Who besides you knows where to turn for necessary information about the family household assets and obligations? Do you have a listing of people who are important contacts, such as tax counselors, attorneys, bankers, brokers, insurance representatives, employers, creditors, and debtors?

• Are you sure titles to property and possessions are held in the best way for all concerned? If not, you may want to ask an estate attorney or a trust officer at your bank for professional assistance.

A good record system will provide a bird's-eye view of what happens to property after you die or when a member of your household dies. Other changes can alter plans too--for example, divorce or separation, children reaching legal age, a long illness, a lawsuit, a natural disaster, loss of a job, and retirement.

What happens if the place where you live is burglarized or there's a fire and records are destroyed? What do you do when you lose track of important papers? Which can be replaced, and how do you go about that? Which ones cannot be replaced, and what do you do about those?

Papers to Keep in Safe Deposit Boxes

Every family household has some important records. Each of us should have a birth certificate or an acceptable substitute. Since there are many occasions when the information on your birth certificate will be needed, it is important that you keep it in a safe place, preferably in a safe deposit box.

If you have lost or misplaced birth certificates, consider applying for replacements now, before there is a pressing need. Otherwise, you may have to wait for one you need quickly.

State registration of births has been mandatory since 1920, and you can contact your State agency to get a copy. The Bureau of the Census also will search its files for proof of age.

By the same token, there will be death certificate for every person someday. These will be needed occasionally and also are best kept in a safe deposit box.

Other important documents to be kept in your safe deposit box include marriage certificates, divorce or other legal papers regarding dissolution of marriage, adoption papers, citizenship records, service papers, and any other document that is either government or court recorded.

The original copy of a will, in most cases, is kept in the safe of the attorney who prepared it. This is highly desirable, since it may save complications later. The client receives two carbon copies, one of which may be put into his or her own safe deposit box. However, there could be a legal delay in getting this copy at his or her death. The third copy, therefore, should be kept at home where it is readily accessible.

Some of your important papers, such as Certificates for securities, which are nonnegotiable (can't be sold or legally transferred) until they are signed by the owner should be maintained

120

in the safe deposit box. Nevertheless, such certificates can be lost or stolen, and the signature can be forged. In either case, replacement involves both cost and delay. Government bonds can be replaced without cost, but there will be a delay of several months. So it is best to keep these in the box also. Among other investment-type documents that require safekeeping are papers that serve as proof of ownership, such as deeds for real estate, other mortgage papers, contracts, automobile titles (if this applies in your State), leases, notes, and such special papers as patents and copyrights.

Renting a Safe Deposit Box

If you don't have a safe deposit box, then consider getting one. The yearly rental, at your bank or financial institution, is inexpensive. Often the smallest size is adequate, though larger sizes are available at slightly higher charges. If you do have a safe deposit box, ask yourself if it is large enough to hold everything that should be in it- and small enough to keep out things that don't need to be there. If you store documents from investment properties or securities, the rental can be claimed as a deduction for income tax purposes. The box should not be used as a catchall for souvenirs and unimportant papers.

What Goes In and What Stays Out of the Safe Deposit Box

A guideline as to what goes in and what stays out of your safe deposit box might be "Put it in if you can't replace it or if it would be costly or troublesome to replace". Many items can, however, be replaced rather easily. Copies of insurance policies can be obtained from your insurance companies. Copies of cancelled checks are usually available at your bank for up to seven years. We recommend you contact your bank to understand the cost involved and the time limit for the availability of your bank records with that particular financial institution. Different institutions will charge and maintain records differently. Generally speaking, you do not need to keep the following in a safe deposit box: income tax returns, education records, employment records, bankbooks, social security cards, guarantees, and burial instructions.

We recommend you make copies of the original items stored in the safe deposit box as well as family heir items. These copies should be stored in a "family heritage dead file". Also in this file you should include your family's obituaries, photos and anything you want to pass to the next generation when the time comes. Be sure to mark the copied items from the safe deposit box as COPY so as not to be confused with the originals. Managing the family affairs should never be overlooked. Today with multiple family components one family may have several lineages which mean several family heritage dead files.

Keeping Tax Records

How long should you keep tax records? The Internal Revenue Service has 3 years in which to audit Federal income tax returns from the date the return was actually filed. However, this limit does not apply in unusual cases. If you failed to report more than 25 percent of your gross income, the Internal Revenue Service has 6 years to collect the tax or to start legal proceedings. Also, there is no statute of limitation if you filed a fraudulent return or if you failed to file a return. But you don't have to keep everything for tax purposes. You can lighten your record load by discarding certain checks and bills once they have served their purpose. For example, you can throw away weekly or monthly salary statements--assuming you are paid in that way--after you check and reconcile them against your annual W-2 Form for the year. We do, however, highly recommend you keep the last pay check stub based on certain deductions and items which do not appear on your Form W-2 (Contributions, Insurances, Retirement transactions, Exemptions, Child Support Payments or other garnishments etc.) but save cancelled checks that relate directly to an entry on your tax return. Also, you need to keep all medical bills for 3 years to back up your cancelled checks.

The Internal Revenue Service generally keeps records forever, although older years may not be available to you as a taxpayer. You can obtain a copy of a certain recent tax return by writing to the Internal Revenue Service and completing Form 4506. Include your check made out to the center to which your return was sent. Make sure you include your social security number and a signature.

We recommend you maintain your income tax returns and supporting documentation forever. Having this information will help you to keep track of your financial highway. Remember, you cannot know where you are going if you do not know where you came from. In addition, if/when you reach 62 or 65 years of age and it is time for you to draw Social Security benefits, there are missing years, the only way to prove your income is by producing a copy of the tax return filed, and some supporting documents, with the Internal Revenue Service for that year.

Making Business and Household Inventory Records

Among your important papers keep an office and household inventory. If there is a fire or burglary in your business or home, these records will help you remember what has to be replaced and how much each item is worth. An inventory also may show that you need to increase your insurance because your possessions are worth more than you thought.

The best way to go about compiling a household inventory is to start with a sheet of paper for each room in your office, house or apartment, etc. Forms on which to record items are available from several places, sometimes from your county's Extension office. We recommend preparing a video of all areas in an organized manner verbally describing certain items and locations to include north, south, east and west.

When you prepare your inventory summaries, start at one point in the room and go all the way around, listing everything, or do the same with the video or camera. For each item, list what it is, how much it cost, when it was purchased, and what it would possibly be worth in the future. If the item was transferred from another family member, be sure to include that information as well. If you take pictures of the rooms and your household possessions, it will make identification or replacement easier. Arrange expensive collections, silver, and jewelry separately and take close-up pictures.

When you have finished inventorying all the rooms, including the basement, garage and attic, add up the total replacement cost. That figure will represent what your personal property and household is worth and is what your insurance should cover. Update your inventory every 6 months or so by adding new purchases and adjusting replacement costs. You may want to have a certified appraisal on certain items for which you have no idea as to the value.

Businesses should maintain their assets in a "Fixed Asset and Depreciation Schedule". This schedule should be updated annually by your accountant and submitted to you with your financial reports and records at the end of the year. The accountant will update this with new assets purchased and the assets which have be retired from use or sold. Remember you will need to provide your accountant with specifics to have your schedules accurate.

Many families have a person or two who archive the heir or heritage of the entire family. These individuals have a greater task of preparing inventories which will need to be passed down to the next generation. When preparing your inventory list be sure to note the following information:

- From which family member did the item initially come?
- Did that member purchase, barter, or receive the item from another family member?
- If purchased, list the date, the store or person purchased from and a description of the item in detail.
- What was the original cost?
- Is a copy of the receipt available and attached?
- Is there a picture or video of the item attached?
- Has an appraisal been done on the item and is the appraisal with the inventory ledger?

The family records need to be thoroughly maintained and updated as time moves forward. Therefore, the individual who chooses to take the task on becomes the family "go to" person and carries a good responsibility for the family.

Organizing an Office or Home Filing System

A system for personal records is a necessity. No matter how modest your home facilities might be, you need a special place to keep your papers. That could be as elaborate as a room or home office or as simple as a corner of the kitchen, bedroom, or hall.

Records, regardless of the filing system used, should be reviewed at least once a year to discard items no longer needed. January is a good time for an overhaul, since it's just before you begin to work on taxes.

The equipment you will need doesn't have to be elaborate. Think about a filing cabinet before you think about a desk. The two-drawer type can be covered with paint or wallpaper. A wooden slab or hollow-core door stretched across the top of two cabinets can make a practical home office desk.

If you don't have space for a small cabinet, buy accordion folders, a storage chest that fits under the bed, or get sturdy cardboard boxes of an appropriate size.

A home computer or portable typewriter and a pocket calculator can be handy, but they are not essential. The essential thing is to know where everything is.

Maintain More Than One File

You should keep two office and two home files, in addition to your safe deposit box at the bank. These two files are your active file and your dead storage file. Your active file will hold:

1) Unpaid bills until paid
2) Paid bill receipts
3) Current bank statements
4) Current cancelled checks
5) Income tax working papers
6) After 3 years, move these items to your dead storage file
7) Businesses will have much more information in their active files based on having many more deductions for tax and financial purposes.

There are other items which should always be kept in your active file. These include:

1) Employment records, such as resumes, recommendation letters and health benefits information
2) Credit card information, including the number of each card by company name

3) Insurance policies
4) Copies of wills
5) Family health records
6) Appliance manuals and warranties
7) Education information, such as transcripts, diplomas, etc.
8) Social Security information on benefits and regulations and
9) An inventory of what's in your safe deposit box (you might store a key in the inventory folder).

Finally, keep a record book or ledger of the whereabouts of your important papers. If you use a loose-leaf binder, you will be able to change papers easily or copy a page or two when the need arises. Some people who have tech skills can implement their system in a spreadsheet and update the schedules to be inserted into the hard copy book or ledger. The book should contain a list of all your savings and checking accounts with bank name, account number and names listed on the accounts. This way you won't become one of the missing depositors who have forgotten their accounts or who have died without telling relatives about them. Also, include the name and branch of the bank where you keep your safe deposit box.

The book also should have all of the family members' social security numbers, and all of the insurance policy information. It's a good idea to keep a copy of your household inventory here as well.

Don't forget to record all your household improvements here because when you sell or transfer your home to another family member, you will be eligible for up to $250,000 waiver of gain on the sale of your personal residence. Home improvements will be added to your cost to determine your "basis value" in your home, which is used for this calculation. If you used credit cards for purchases, we suggest you keep the credit card statement and the actual receipt. Be sure to write on the receipt the pertinent information, as many of the store receipts will fade away over a period of time. We also recommend you scan the receipts, if significant, into the computer and label it as an XXXX.pdf file with a proper and relative name.

We recommend you retain all relevant information related to real estate and vehicles for at least up to five (5) years after the asset has been sold or retired. For as long as you own the item, we recommend you maintain all repair, renovation, upgrades and custom add-ons to add to your cost/basis for when the property is transferred.

Finally, make sure someone else knows and understands the business and the family's record-keeping system.

Things to Remember

Use the checklist chart below to remind yourself what to keep and what you can discard.

Safe Deposit Box

1. Birth Certificates
2. Citizenship Papers
3. Marriage Certificates
4. Adoption Papers
5. Divorce Decrees
6. Wills
7. Death Certificates
8. Deeds
9. Titles to Automobiles
10. Household Inventory – Main Ledger/Book
11. Veteran's Papers
12. Bonds and Stock Certificates
13. Important Contracts, including original retirement items – IRA, SEP, 401-K etc.
14. Jewelry not worn on a regular basis

Active File

1. Tax Receipts
2. Unpaid Bills
3. Paid Bill Receipts
4. Current Bank Statements
5. Current Cancelled Checks
6. Income Tax Working Papers
7. Employment Records
8. Health Benefits Information
9. Annual Retirement Information
10. Credit Card Information
11. Insurance Policies

12. Copies of Wills
13. Family Health Records
14. Appliance Manuals and Warranties
15. Receipts of Items Under Warranty
16. Education Information
17. Inventory of Safe Deposit Box (and key)
18. Loan Statements
19. Loan Payment Books
20. Receipts of Expensive Items Not Yet Paid For

Dead Storage

All Active File Papers over 3 years old should be moved to an area for safe storage. Plastic bins or boxes with tops should be labeled and placed in a secure area for long-term storage. Many of your more intense items will fit in one bin for multiple years. You will be amazed at the amount of space you have once you have gotten your records and items organized. If you store these records in a basement or low area, be sure not to put your materials on the floor but install shelving to place them on to protect them just in case of flooding.

Items to Discard

1. Utility bills, phone bills unless in business
2. Cancelled checks for cash or nondeductible Expenses
3. Expired warranties
4. Coupons after expiration date
5. Any mail for which you have no interest or will not act on in the next 30 days
6. All envelopes which your bills come in and any additional advertising not relevant to your circumstances.

Be sure to review our "Summary of Storing tax records: How long is long enough?" in the back of this publication.

S.Y.N.C. 16

Checklist Summary of your Progress

Rule for Success

In Closing

There is one final bit of advice which I believe is vital to your mental, spiritual health and well-being. To be successful in the best and broadest sense of that word, to achieve a full and rich and satisfying life, you must banish all hate. Leave no room in your heart for hate. Hate is a cancer which eats away all that is good. There will be times when you think hate is justified, when hate is almost impossible to avoid. For there is meanness in the world, and prejudice and unkindness. Even so, you must turn away hate, and rise above hate, for hate will injure you most of all and in the end it will consume and destroy you.

Chapter 16

Checklist Summary of your Progress

Now that you have decided you are definitely going into your business, you have talked to those important people in your life, you are totally committed and there is no stopping you, let's get you started down this road to success.

Describe your new business idea_____

Name for your business_____

Address for your business_____

Location for your business activity_____

Telephone numbers for the business_____

Determined your Organizational Structure_____

_____

Contact your Accountant for assistance at this point; name and phone
_____

Apply for your Employer Identification Number _____

Contact your Banker for assistance; name and phone #

_____

Contact your Attorney for assistance; name and phone #

_____

Open your business bank
account_____

Determine your accounting system to be used in keeping track of all your investing and operational activities

_____

Apply for your Business Tax Licenses_____

Apply for your Sales Tax Number with your State Department of Revenue _____

Obtain the proper insurance coverage for your industry
_____
List your insurance agency, phone number and policy number here.

Set up your Self Employee Pension (SEP/IRA) account for depositing your retirement funds for income tax diversion.   You can fund these accounts up to your tax return deadlines.

_____

Prepare an inventory of assets to be transferred into your new or existing business_____

   We recommend you set up a three ring binder for copies of your original correspondence from the various team members and tax authorities with a copy of this sheet to write the information above in summary form for future reference and business planning.

S.Y.N.C. 17

S.Y.N.C., We Are Almost There

There is no stopping you now.

Let's continue on your road to success!

Rule for Success

ACHIEVEMENT

Every victory empowers your heart
to shape your destiny.

Chapter 17

S.Y.N.C., We Are Almost There

This section will give you more details to assist you with the previous checklist. These details will give you the reasons for various recommendations which can always be upgraded as your business develops and grows.

Name for your business_____
If you have several new projects in mind you may want to have a generic name for your business with divisions for income and cost analysis down the road.

Address for your business_____
We suggest you obtain a Post Office Box to avoid the commingling of your personal mail with the business mail. This also will allow a look of being professional at a very low cost. In addition, your mail will be secure and possibly delivered timelier. It allows you to have some anonymity. This is only temporary until you make a decision to get an office location with your branding or long-term for the protection of your correspondence.

Location for your business activity_____

Telephone numbers for the business_____
Many people are using their cell phones to communicate at all times with all persons. We recommend you have at least one land line available for very important calls which you would never want to drop or have telephone issues. In today's competitive telephone system wars, you could obtain a very good land line for under $30.00 per month. Investigate all options and be sure to make notes of features. Ask yourself, do I really need call waiting on my land line or conference calling? The single land line could double as a land-based fax line with technology which would sort the calls appropriately.

S.Y.N.C.

Determined your Organizational Structure_____

Contact your Accountant for assistance from this point

Determine your accounting system to be used in keeping track of all your investing and operational activities

See our section on Accounting / Bookkeeping section of this publication.

Apply for your Federal Employer Identification Number ((F)EIN)

The Internal Revenue Service is the only organization which issues this number. Many people confuse this number with their Sales Tax Number, which we will discuss later. The Internal Revenue Service has improved their processing methods and makes it relatively easy to obtain this number. We suggest you complete your Form SS-4 completely and be sure to retain a copy in your permanent section of business book for future reference. If you have a question about any of this; STOP and call a professional for assistance. Applying for this number is like obtaining a Social Security Number for your business. After all, this is your new baby. You as an individual will ever only need one FEIN #. If your business changes its organizational structure, you should contact the IRS for advice on how to convert your current FEIN# to the new business or a different venture. If you do not want to use your social security number to identify your business, you should obtain a Federal Employer Identification Number ((F)EIN) from the Internal Revenue Service. The FEIN is your business's permanent identification number and can be used for most of your business needs including: opening a bank account, applying for business licenses and filing a tax return by mail. We do not recommend you apply for your FEIN without prior knowledge of understanding the form and what you are doing, however, you can obtain information and register for your FEIN online at www.irs.gov or by calling 1-800-829-4933. All corporations and partnerships are required to have an FEIN. Apply for your Business Tax Licenses_____.

S.Y.N.C.

Many cities and states require you to have a license to do business in their areas. At this point you should have researched the requirements of your locality to determine the licenses required for you to operate your business in your particular area. If at any time you feel you have not gotten all the information in this area, then we suggest you start making phone calls to the various tax authorities until it becomes clear. Nashville requires both a city and county business tax license. The first year's fees are usually standard amounts. The following years annual reports are usually based on your company's gross sales, less any personal property taxes paid during that year. Rates and classes vary depending upon your particular industry.

Apply for your Sales Tax Number with your State Department of Revenue _____.
This number will be used for purchasing your materials used in the production of any products with no sales tax cost. Once you sell a product, you will be responsible for collecting the sales tax and remitting the collected sales tax on to your State's Department of Revenue.

Obtain the proper insurance coverage for your industry.

_____

Some industries do not require you to obtain additional insurances; however, we strongly recommend you consult with a qualified Insurance Agent to review your future business and the possibility of needing coverage. One example is if you purchase a box truck and decide to hire a driver to do local deliveries for your company. Will the standard insurance cover the driver, the load and any other incidents which may occur while the vehicle is in working operation? Or, you may be working on a specific professional scientific project for a client and inadvertently overlook an important task, but you have completed the project, submitted it and have received payment. The client finds the error and states it will cost their company a huge amount of money which they want you to cover. (Even if you had an organizational structure other than a Sole Proprietorship, you could still be held accountable and liable.)

S.Y.N.C.

Open your business bank account_____
Instructions on this process are included in the Business Banking
Procedure section of this publication.

Set up your Simplified Employee Pension Plan (SEP/IRA) account
for depositing your retirement funds for income tax diversion. You
will be able to deposit and deduct on your tax return a contribution
equivalent to a percentage of your net profit/earnings from your self-
employment activity. You also will be able to deposit funds through
all extension deadlines – October 15 of each year for the previous
year. We recommend you invest your funds into a retirement money
market account unless you have knowledge of the stock market and
mutual funds or you hire a financial broker. All employees are
eligible for the company's SEP Plan.

_____

Prepare an inventory of assets to be transferred into your new or
existing business. Complete the listing of assets owned prior to
starting your new business and purchased prior to this year-end.

Some assets and reference materials owned prior to starting your
business may be eligible to be used as an initial investment into your
business if they have never been recorded in the past and have not
been depreciated on your books and income taxes. Many accountants
overlook these items with startups and clients are not familiar with
fixed asset management. One example would be medical
professionals reference materials and equipment required to be
purchased and used prior to setting up their medical offices. The
listing of new or used furniture, equipment and assets should include
the following information: description of asset, date acquired, make,
model, serial number, cost, and a copy of invoice when purchased and
photo if available.

_____

Please note on the lines available if the step has been completed or
any important numbers you may need to reference in the future.

Be sure to review our Checklist of Necessary Business Documents for
Financial Statements and Income Tax Preparation in the back of this
publication

S.Y.N.C.

136

S.Y.N.C. 18

Resources Guide

Rule for Success

ENDURANCE

The glory is not in ever failing;
but in the rising every time you fail…

Chapter 18

Resources Guide

U. S. Tax Services – Mamie A. Brinkley
http://www.ustaxservices.com/

Internal Revenue Service Individual Videos
http://www.irsvideos.gov/Individual

Score (Service Core of Retired Executives)
http://www.score.org/
http://www.scorenashville.org/

Internal Revenue Service - Small Business Taxpayer--
http://www.irsvideos.gov/SmallBusinessTaxpayer/virtualworkshop/

North American Industry Classification System (NAICS) and Job Classifications and Descriptions
http://www.bls.gov/bls/naics.htm

The Small Business School http://www.smallbusinessschool.org/

Office Depot Business Tools
http://www.officedepot.com/a/businesstools/sbh/default/
http://www.officedepot.com/a/business-resource-center/

Printable Calendars
http://www.printablecalendar.ca/

EHow on How to Do just about anything
http://www.ehow.com/info/

State of Tennessee Smart Business Guide
http://www.tn.gov/ecd/bero/pdf/TNSmartStartGuide.pdf

Welcome to EFTPS®   https://www.eftps.gov/eftps/
(This site is for paying Internal Revenue Service income tax liabilities.)

The United States Patent and Trademark Office

http://www.uspto.gov/

United States Copyright Office   http://www.copyright.gov/

You or a Family Member may have Unclaimed Property

http://www.Unclaimed.org

http://www.MissingMoney.com

Where to Write for Vital Records

http://www.cdc.gov/nchs/howto/w2w/w2welcom.htm

S.Y.N.C. 19

Reference Materials and Checklist

Rule for Success

SERENITY

Serenity is taking a deep breath before taking the next big step.

Reference Materials and Checklists

Page #

The Entrepreneur's Quiz

ANSWERS

1.	a	oldest
2.	a	married
3.	a	man
4.	c	thirties
5.	a	teens
6.	d	master's degree
7.	b	can't work for anyone else
8.	c	father
9.	b	chair
10.	b	luck/blessings
11.	d	are in secret conflict
12.	b	external management professionals
13.	d	doers
14.	b	moderate risk takers
15.	b	a customer

Number of Questions Answered Correctly	Score
11 or more	Successful Entrepreneur
10 - 11	Entrepreneur
9 - 10	Latent Entrepreneur
8 - 9	Potential Entrepreneur
7 - 8	Borderline Entrepreneur
7 or less	Hired Hand

This is just a whimsical task to get you to thinking. No actual grading system has been documented. The answers you choose do not necessarily lend to whether your business will be successful. Just reflect on your answers and determine if your mind is in the right place to be an entrepreneur and be sure to follow your passion.

S.Y.N.C.

U. S. Tax Services
615.333.3330

Checklist for Individual Income Tax Preparation

Please submit receipts and documentation for items **you** checked below **with your** accurate adding machine tapes **or summarized spreadsheet, along with this c**hecklist at the time of your appointment.

_____Accounting/Tax Preparation Fees
_____Adoption Expenses and Fees
_____Alimony Paid or Received-Ex-Spouse SS #
_____**Appointment for Personal Financial Planning**
_____Bad Debt with Documentation
_____Bankruptcy Filed in _____
    Chapter 7 _____ Chapter 13_____
_____Business Miles Relating to Job Activity--
    Log Required, Total miles for year &
    Description of Vehicle
_____Business Operation Activity Summary
_____Business Publications
_____Cancellation of Debt – Form 1099-C
_____Capital Gain/Losses on Sale of Stocks/Mutual Funds
    (Form 1099-B)
_____Casualty and Theft Losses
_____Change of Home Address
_____Change of Telephone Numbers
_____Charitable Contributions & Transportation
_____Child Born in current year
_____Child Care Expenses
_____Child Support Payments
_____Children's Full Name, Copy of S.S. Card & DOB
_____Dependent children age 19 or over (income & occupation
    information)
_____Closing Papers on Refinancing of Home
_____Drivers License-Copy of Current
_____Dividend Income (Form 1099 DIV's)

_____Earnings from Coverdell education savings account
        Nontaxable or distribution from the account
_____Educational/Higher Learning Tuition (Form 1098-T)
_____Educator's expenses and reimbursements (Teachers))
_____Electric or clean-fuel Vehicle placed in service
_____Electronic Filing for Direct Deposit (copy of blank
        check or savings acct info)
_____Employment Fees Paid Out by You
_____Energy credit for residential qualified energy efficiency
        improvement
_____Estimated Tax Payments, Dates and Ck #'s (Copy)
_____Farm Income/Expenses
_____Federal Income Tax Withheld (W-2, 1099,etc)
_____Foreclosures on Real Estate
_____Foreign Country Activity
_____Gambling Winnings (Form W-2G) and Losses
_____Health Savings Account Contributions/Disbursements
_____Home Office Expenses
_____In-transit Miles (Between Jobs)
_____Income Taxes for State or Local Governments
_____Income from Trust/Estates (Sch. K-1's)
_____IRA, Roth (Nondeductible), Check your Max contribution
        for each year and provide Form 5498 (Year End
        Summary)
_____Interest Income (Form 1099-INT's)
_____Last Pay Check Stub
_____Long-term care insurance premium paid
_____Marital Status Changes
_____Medical Health/Archer Savings Accounts
_____Medical Insurance Paid (Self Employed = 100%)
_____Medical and Dental Expenses
_____Medical Transportation
_____Medicare Income or Expenses
_____Mortgage Interest Paid (incl. Equity Loan)-Form 1098
_____Moving Expenses (Over 50 Miles)
_____Other Income (Form 1099-MISC's)
_____Partnership/Corporation (Schedule K-1's)
_____Pension/Annuity Income/Expenses (1099 R)
_____Personal Property Taxes
_____Points-paid on the purchase/refinance of real estate
        (Settlement Paperwork)

_____Purchase of motor vehicle, boat or Home Renovations
_____Real Estate Property Taxes
_____Real Estate Transactions – Related Closing Stmts.
     (Acquisition, Refinance or Sale)
_____Rental Property Activity
_____Safe Deposit Box
_____Salaries (Form W-2's)
_____Sale/Exchange Property (including residence,
     Form 1099-s)
_____Sales Tax Deduction on Large Purchases (Automobile)
_____SEP, SIMPLE Retirement Plan Contributions
_____State/Local Tax Refunds (Form 1099-G) or Credits
_____Small Tools Used for Work not paid for by Employer
_____Social Security Income/Expenses – (Form SSA 1099)
_____Student Loans interest paid and terms (Up to
     $2,500.00, Form 1098-E)
_____Unemployment Compensation
_____Uniform Expenses/Maintenance
_____Union and Professional Dues
_____Worthless Securities/Debts
_____IRS Web site - _www.irs.gov_
_____**Any other tax forms or information that you may have
     received**
_____CAN SOMEONE CLAIM YOU AS A DEPENDENT?
_____ Do you need an organizer for this year?
_____ Are you a client from last year?
_____**Correspondence from Internal Revenue Service or State
Department of Revenues**

The **DEADLINE** for filing Form 1040 U. S. Individual
Income Tax Return is April 15, unless this day falls on a
weekend or holiday

**Office Location: 2948 Nolensville Pike
Nashville, Tennessee 37211-2339**

If this is your first year using our firm, please provide us with copies of the previous
THREE (3) years tax returns you filed.

"Thank you for allowing us to provide services to you, your family and friends"

U. S. Tax Services
615.333.3330

Checklist of Necessary Business Documents for Financial Statements and Income Tax Preparation

A. Bank statements, Canceled Checks, debit and credit memos, automatic drafts, overdraft   notices and etc. # of Month Submitted

B. Duplicate Deposit Book (s) or Deposit Tickets (CRJ and Summary)

C. Check Disbursement Journal sheets for one-write systems - Check Stubs or Register to prepare CDJ and Summary

D. Accounts Receivable Day Sheets or Daily Record Logs of Sales/Income operating activity (Totaled & Summarized)

E. Sales Tax Reports and all Subsequent Memorandums

F. Cash Paid Receipts for any other expenses paid by cash or a personal check instead of a business check

G. Home Office expenses, provide total square feet of building and square feet of office

H. Home Office Expenses used for business purposes (ex. Rent, Gas, Electricity, Property Taxes, Insurance, Repairs, Water, Interest Expense, etc.)

I. Inventory on hand of Merchandise– beginning and ending of each year

J. Auto Expenses (Mileage, interest, repairs, insurance, parking, etc). A log/file should be maintained with the detail for each vehicle & description

K. Also a List of full-time Employees, Sub contractors, and/or Temporary
   a. Employees with current addresses and social security number,
   b. along with the following quarterly and annual Payroll Reports including:
      1. Form 941's
      2. Form 940
      3. State Unemployment Reports

4. Form W-2's and W-3
5. Form 1099's and 1096
6. Form W-4 or W-9 Each Person

L. All information pertaining to any loans you have with financial institutions or from other sources, statements for interest expense and principal balances as of the end of each year paid along with original loan agreements or settlement sheets

M. Credit Card Statements used in Business along with signed receipts for purchases

N. Copies of Lease agreements for space, equipment and automobiles

O. Copies of Deeds, closing statements and mortgages on real estate

P. Complete Listing of assets owned prior to starting your business and this prior to this year-end. Some assets and reference materials will be eligible as an initial investment into your business if they have never been recorded in the past and depreciated on your income taxes. Many accountants overlook these deduction and clients are not familiar with fixed asset management. One example would be medical professionals reference materials and equipment required to be purchased and used prior to setting up an medical office.

Q. Copies of business tax licenses

R. Personality tax forms

S. Listing of new or used furniture, equipment and assets acquired in current year, along with description of asset, date acquired, make, model, serial number, cost, and a copy of invoice when purchased

T. Copy of Corporate Charter, Board Minutes and Officers or Owners personal information including name, address, SS # and telephone #

U. Copy of last three years of Individual and Business Tax returns Filed
   a. Individual Form 1040 Schedule C
   b. Partnership Form 1065 and all Attachments
   c. Corporate Form 1120 or 1120S depending on corporate status

V. All Notices from Internal Revenue Service, State Tax and Local Authorities

We are aware that the information listed above may or may not pertain to your business.

Please review this list thoroughly & bring to our office all pertinent information relating to your business transactions. We do not prepare business financial statements and income tax returns without documentation.

Please provide us with copies of your last three years income tax returns to ensure consistency, if not already on file.

Thank God----every morning when you get up----that you have something to do which must be done, whether you like it or not.

Being forced to work, and forced to do your best, will breed in you a hundred virtues that the idle never know.
(Unknown author)

2948 Nolensville Pike, Nashville, Tennessee 37211-2339

Mamie Brinkley

www.ustaxservices.com

info@ustaxservices.com

U. S. Tax Services
615.333.3330

www.ustaxservices.com   info@ustaxservices.com

Detail list of Expenses to Consider as Business Deductions

Air Fare
Alarm Clock
Antenna
Amour-All
Atlas
ATM Fees
Auto Mileage
Batteries
Bedroll
Ben Gay
Boot Repair
Boots (Steel-Toed & Work Rubber)
Briefcase
Broom & Dustpan
Buffer to Shine
Bunk Heater & Fan
Cash Paid Receipts for Various Items
Cc Curtains
Cab Fare
Calculator
Camera(s)
Car Rental
CB Radio
CB Repair
CDL Driver License
Cellular Phone
Cellular/Wireless Fees
Check Cashing Fees
Circuit Tester
Claims for Damages
Cleaning & Detailing
Cleaning Supplies (Clorox, De-greaser)
Clip Board
Coffee Maker
Com-check Fees
Computer Software and Accessories
Contract Labor (Lumper Fees)
Cooler/Cooler Motor
Copies
Credit Card Charges

Credit Reports
Crowbar
Decontamination
De-Icer
Digital Devices Used in Business
Disinfectant
Dot Physical
Dry Cleaning
Duct Tape
Electrical Tape
Ether
Eyewear (Sun, Safety, Reading)
Fan Clamps
Faxes & Fees
Film Development
Film for Camera
Finance Charges
First Aid Supplies
Flags
Flares
Flashlights
Flyswatter
Fuel & Fluids
Gatorade (Hydration)
GPS System
Hand Cleaner
Hangers
Hard Hat
Hazmat Gear
Hearing Aids
Home Office Expenses
Hotel/Motels Expenses Paid
Ice
Incidentals
Insurance
Internet Services
Jack Straps
Lap Desk
Laundry Bag
Laundry Soap
Limousine or Taxi Services

Load Chains
Locks
Lodging
Log Book Covers
Log Books
Lot Lizard Repellent
Magnifying Glass
Maintenance, Parts & Repairs
Map Lamp
Maps
Meal per Diem *Bonus
Meals
Money Order Fees
Monitors of Cameras
Office Equipment
Office Furniture
Office Supplies (Liquid Paper, Notebook Paper, Pens, Pencils, Stapler, Staples)
Overnights for the Year (per Scheduler or Logbook)
Paper Towels
Parking Fees
Performance Wardrobe
Pillows
Portable Radio
Portable Television
Portable Vacuum
Power Booster
Power Cords
Radio Equipment & Accessories
Rain Gear
Razors
Reefer Fuels
Refrigerator
Reimbursement for Meals, Entertainment & Incidentals
Road Use Taxes (Form 2290)
Safety Devices

Sauce Pans
Sett Covers
Sewing Kit
Shaving Tote
Sheets & Linens
Shift Grip
Showers
Signage Expense
State Road Use Taxes Paid
Storage Fees
Tarps
Thermal Underwear
Thermos Bottle
Time Pieces (Wrist Watch, Stop Watches)
Tire Iron
Tires & Rims Purchases
Tissues
Toaster
Toiletries
Tolls
Tools
Towels
Towing
Trash Bags & Cans
Travel Bags
Tupperware
Uniform Alterations
Uniforms
Uniform Maintenance
Vaseline
Visine
Washing & Waxing
WD-40
Weather-Tracking Systems
Weight Charges & Fees
Window Screen
Work Gloves
Wrist Watch

U. S. Tax Services
615.333.3330

AUTOMOBILE/VEHICLE EXPENSE WORKSHEET

Page 1

Year (s) used in business:_____

Taxpayer's Name: _____
       Occupation:_____

Spouse's Name: _____
       Occupation:_____

What is auto used for? (Check all that apply)

_____ Employer _____ Sch. C _____ Sch. F _____ Moving
_____ Meetings/Job Related   _____ Job to School

_____ Two (2) Jobs   _____ Charitable   _____ Tax Prep/Invest
_____ Rental   _____ Medical   _____ Other

1. Do you own more than one (1) vehicle? ___Yes   ___ No
2. Does your employer provide the vehicle ___Yes   ___ No
3. Are you reimbursed by your employer? ___Yes   ___ No
4. If reimbursed, is the payment included in W-2? ___Yes   ___ No
5. Are your records written or oral?   ___Written   ___Oral

VEHICLE INFORMATION	Vehicle 1	Vehicle 2
Year/make	_____	_____
Date placed in service	_____	_____
Date retired	_____	_____
Purchase price	_____	_____
Selling price .	_____	_____
Trade-in?	_____	_____
Ending odometer reading	_____	_____
Beginning reading .	_____	_____
Total miles	_____	_____
Business miles	_____	_____
Commuting miles	_____	_____
Personal miles	_____	_____
Business use percent	_____	_____

S.Y.N.C.

U. S. Tax Services
615.333.3330

AUTOMOBILE/VEHICLE EXPENSE WORKSHEET

Page 2

EXPENSES (Identify if Monthly (M) or Annually (A))

Gas & oil. . $_____ $ _____
Insurance/auto club   _____   _____
Maintenance and repairs   _____   _____
License (do not include personal property tax)

                                _____   _____
Wash/wax/misc.   _____   _____
Tires/battery   _____   _____
Vehicle rental   _____   _____
Parking/tolls $_____ $_____

Lease Payments – Lien Holder (s) _____

Account #_____   _____

         _____

Total Interest Expense Paid during current year

                                _____   _____

TOTAL $_____ $_____

Miscellaneous Notes _____

Created by Mamie Brinkley

Date Submitted to U. S. Tax Services _____

152

U. S. Tax Services
615.333.3330

Internal Revenue Service Mileage Rates
All rates shown are per mile (p/m)

Year		Business Rates (p/m)	Average cost of gas (per gallon)	Charitable Rates (p/m)	Medical Rates (p/m)	Moving Rates (p/m)
2013		56.5 Cents		14 Cents	24 Cents	24 Cents
2012		55.5 Cents	3.67	14 Cents	23 Cents	23 Cents
2011	Jan - June	51 Cents	3.49	14 Cents	19 Cents	19 Cents
	July- Dec	55.5 Cents	3.46	14 Cents	23.5 Cents	23.5 Cents
2010		50 Cents	2.84	14 Cents	16.5 Cents	16.5 Cents
2009		55 Cents	2.46	14 Cents	24 Cents	24 Cents
2008	Jan - June	50.5 Cents	3.62	14 Cents	19 Cents	19 Cents
	July- Dec	58.5 Cents	3.20	14 Cents	27 Cents	27 Cents
2007		48.5 Cents	2.83	14 Cents	20 Cents	20 Cents
2006		44.5 Cents	2.80	14 Cents	18 Cents	18 Cents

S.Y.N.C.

Year	Period					
2005	Jan - Aug	40.5 Cents	2.70	14 Cents	15 Cents	15 Cents
	Sept - Dec	48.5 Cents		14 Cents	22 Cents	22 Cents
2004		37.5 Cents	2.20	14 Cents	14 Cents	14 Cents
2003		36 Cents	1.90	14 Cents	12 Cents	12 Cents
2002		36.5 Cents	1.70	14 Cents	13 Cents	13 Cents
2001		34.5 Cents	1.90	14 Cents	12 Cents	12 Cents
2000		32.5 Cents	1.80	14 Cents	10 Cents	10 Cents
1999	Jan - Mar	32.5 Cents	1.40	14 Cents	10 Cents	10 Cents
	Apr - Dec	31 Cents		14 Cents	10 Cents	10 Cents
1998		32.5 Cents	1.20	14 Cents	10 Cents	10 Cents
1997		31.2 Cents	1.40	12 Cents	10 Cents	10 Cents

Refer to the following link for updated rates.

http://www.irs.gov/Tax-Professionals/Standard-Mileage-Rates

S.Y.N.C.

Organizational Structure Summary Grid

Organizational Structures Summary
The pros and cons of corporations, LLCs, partnerships, sole proprietorships, and more.

Type of Entity	Main Advantages	Main Drawbacks
Sole Proprietorship	Simple and inexpensive to create and operate, owner reports profit or loss on his or her personal tax return	Owner personally liable for business debts
General Partnership	Simple and inexpensive to create and operate, owners (partners) report their share of profit or loss on their personal tax returns	Owners (partners) personally liable for business debts
Limited Partnership	Limited partners have limited personal liability for business debts as long as they don't participate in management. General partners can raise cash without involving outside investors in management of business	General partners personally liable for business debts More expensive to create than general partnership
Regular Corporation	Owners have limited personal liability for business debts Fringe benefits can be deducted as business expense Owners can split corporate profit among owners and corporation, paying lower overall tax rate	More expensive to create than partnership or sole proprietorship Paperwork can seem burdensome to some owners Separate taxable entity
S Corporation	Owners have limited personal liability for business debts Owners report their share of corporate profit or loss on their personal tax returns Owners can use corporate loss to offset income from other sources	More expensive to create than partnership or sole proprietorship More paperwork than for a limited liability company which offers similar advantages Income must be allocated to owners according to their ownership interests Fringe benefits limited for owners who own more than 2% of shares

S. Y. N. C.

Organizational Structures Summary

The pros and cons of corporations, LLCs, partnerships, sole proprietorships, and more.

Professional Corporation	Owners have no personal liability for malpractice of other owners	More expensive to create than partnership or sole proprietorship
		Paperwork can seem burdensome to some owners
		All owners must belong to the same profession
	Corporation doesn't pay income taxes	Full tax advantages available only to groups organized for charitable, scientific, educational, literary or religious purposes
Nonprofit Corporation	Contributions to charitable corporation are tax-deductible	Property transferred to corporation stays there; if corporation ends, property must go to another nonprofit
	Fringe benefits can be deducted as business expense	
	Owners have limited personal liability for business debts even if they participate in management	More expensive to create than partnership or sole proprietorship
Limited Liability Company	Profit and loss can be allocated differently than ownership interests	State laws for creating LLCs may not reflect latest federal tax changes
	IRS rules now allow LLCs to choose between being taxed as partnership or corporation	Some states require franchise taxes to be paid
Professional Limited Liability Company	Same advantages as a regular limited liability company	Same as for a regular limited liability company
	Gives state licensed professionals a way to enjoy those advantages	Members must all belong to the same profession

Provided by Mamie A. Brinkley Do Not Copy without Permission

S.Y.N.C.

Organizational Structures Summary

The pros and cons of corporations, LLCs, partnerships, sole proprietorships, and more.

Limited Liability Partnership		
Mostly of interest to partners in old line professions such as law, medicine and accounting		Unlike a limited liability company or a professional limited liability company, owners (partners) remain personally liable for many types of obligations owed to business creditors, lenders and landlords
Owners (partners) aren't personally liable for the malpractice of other partners		Not available in all states
Owners report their share of profit or loss on their personal tax returns		Often limited to a short list of professions

S.Y.N.C.

U. S. Tax Services

615.333.3330

Copy of Completed Deposit Slip and Instructions

Sample Deposit Slip

Date of Deposit			0 7. 0 5. 2 0 x x			dollars	cents
Name and description						dollars	cents
Currency						512	
Coins							33
Checks (Enter Separately)						16	00
ABC Company Ck # 12845						1,025	72
Century Appliance Services mo # 589975662543						4,583	94
A. Cash Received from yard sale venture 7/01 $528.33: If a client paid you in cash you would put the clients name and receipt number here and staple your copy of the receipt to the back of the deposit slip remaining in the deposit book.						528	33
Loan Received from World bank: principle amount 15,000.00 payable 180 months @ 9.5% int less fees of 275.00 Bank Check # 6782345-99						14,725	00
Sale of RE at 789 Saxon Drive close date 7/02 SP 50000- Closing cost 27250 - Title Co Check # 78905						22,750	00
Entrepreneur Name Investment from personal funds Check # 12345						3,000	00
*Currency = Cash sales from trade show Receipt copies attached							
Total Deposit						46,612	99

Your Company Name and
Address goes here

Cash + 6 Checks	$ 46,612.99

Number of
items
attached

Total Deposited
Amount

S.Y.N.C.

Instructions for completing deposit tickets

Please be sure to include the Name on each check (from), check # and explanation if not for sales/services.

Use the carbon paper which comes in the back of the deposit book when completing the ticket. Give the carbon copy to the teller and you maintain the original top inked copy. Staple the banks receipt, any check stubs or cash receipts to the back of your original deposit ticket and store in a safe place for the accountant.

*Place a circle around the explanation of the cash to show the bank it is not included a second time in the total

This information provided by
Mamie A. Brinkley, Licensed Public Accountant

S.Y.N.C.

U. S. Tax Services
615.333.3330

Copy of Completed Check and Check Stub and Instructions

Manual Check Stub	Manual Actual Check

			Date of
		Check #	Check -
Check # 55578	Company Name	55578	07.02.20xx
	Company Address		
Date of			
Check 07/02/20xx	City, State and Zip Code		
	Company Telephone Number		
Paid to			
Ajax Suppliers for Invoice # 25687 for 1500 Widgets	Pay to the Order of Ajax Suppliers		$782.23
Begin	Seven Hundred Eighty Two and 23/100xxxxxxxxxxxxx-----		
Balance 7,922.17	Dollars		
Amount of			
Check 782.23			
Ending			
Balanc			
e 7,139.44			
	For 1500 Widgets Invoice # 25687		
Deposit			Signat
7/1/xx 46,612.99	(Purpose of Payment)		ures
	(Magnetic codes)		
Beg	Bank Routing # 9	Ck #	Account Number
Bal 53,752.93	digits	xxxx	xxxxxxxxxx

When writing manual checks, always complete the stub first, then the actual check. Please be descriptive so that when updating the accounting system, proper coding and classification can be done with each check. In some cases we recommend you use a three (3) or seven (7) ring binder check, thereby allowing you to take a group of checks along with the check stubs to be completed as you need to write a check. Of course the stubs would need to be put back in the check book once used so the Accountant can update your financial records. It may also be helpful to tape any receipts, obtained for your purchase, to the back of the stubs for more detail.

Most banking institutions have opted to reduce their cost by not supplying you with copies or original checks after processing monthly via their systems. However, if you are a business professional, you should insist the bank provide you with this information and pay the additional $10.00-$20.00 monthly fee, if applicable. The reason for this requirement, if you are ever audited and the IRS wants to see actual transactions; the bank will certainly charge you for research and copies which could have a significant cost and time. Many of the banks will only retrieve your information for seven (7) or less years.

The smaller micro images are *not acceptable* based on the difficulty in reading and having to use a magnifying glass to read these smaller images. Be sure to request the larger four (4) checks on a page image, which also provides you both the front and back of the checks processed. This is one of those matters that you should take seriously, as you pay now or pay more latter.

Internal Revenue Service has up to 3 years from the date a return is filed to request a review/audit of your records and tax return filed. The alternative option to this is to go online and print the front and back of all transactions to your computer or hard copy. As you can tell, this method would take quite a bit of ink and time which could be just as costly if not more costly. Once the bank has begun to print the larger 4 on a page checks, many of them will allow you to download these statements into an Adobe File which works just as well.

This information provided by

Mamie A. Brinkley, Licensed Public Accountant

S.Y.N.C.

Summary of Storing Records:
How long is long enough?

Federal law requires you to maintain copies of your tax returns and supporting documents for three years. This is called the "three-year law" and leads many people to believe they're safe provided they retain their documents for this period of time.

However, if the IRS believes you have significantly underreported your income (by 25 percent or more), or believes there may be indication of fraud; it may go back six years in an audit. To be safe, use the following guidelines.

Business Records To Keep...	Personal Records To Keep...
1 Year	1 Year
3 Years	3 Years
6 Years	6 Years
Forever	Forever

Special Circumstances

Caution: Identity theft is a serious threat in today's world, and it is important to take every precaution to avoid it. After it is no longer necessary to retain your tax records, financial statements, or any other documents with your personal information, you should dispose of these records by shredding them and not disposing of them by merely throwing them away in the trash.

Business Documents To Keep For One Year

- Correspondence with Customers and Vendors
- Duplicate Deposit Slips
- Purchase Orders (other than Purchasing Department copy)
- Receiving Sheets
- Requisitions
- Stenographer's Notebooks
- Stockroom Withdrawal Forms

Business Documents To Keep For Three Years

- Employee Personnel Records (after termination)
- Employment Applications
- Expired Insurance Policies
- General Correspondence
- Internal Audit Reports
- Internal Reports
- Petty Cash Vouchers
- Physical Inventory Tags
- Savings Bond Registration Records of Employees
- Time Cards For Hourly Employees

Business Documents To Keep For Six Years

- Accident Reports, Claims
- Accounts Payable Ledgers and Schedules
- Accounts Receivable Ledgers and Schedules
- Bank Statements and Reconciliations
- Cancelled Checks
- Cancelled Stock and Bond Certificates
- Employment Tax Records
- Expense Analysis and Expense Distribution Schedules
- Expired Contracts, Leases
- Expired Option Records
- Inventories of Products, Materials, Supplies
- Invoices to Customers
- Notes Receivable Ledgers, Schedules

- Payroll Records and Summaries, including payment to pensioners
- Plant Cost Ledgers
- Purchasing Department Copies of Purchase Orders
- Sales Records
- Subsidiary Ledgers
- Time Books
- Travel and Entertainment Records
- Vouchers for Payments to Vendors, Employees, etc.
- Voucher Register, Schedules

Business Records To Keep Forever

While federal guidelines do not require you to keep tax records "forever," in many cases there will be other reasons you'll want to retain these documents indefinitely.

- Audit Reports from CPAs/Accountants
- Cancelled Checks for Important Payments (especially tax payments)
- Cash Books, Charts of Accounts
- Contracts, Leases Currently in Effect
- Corporate Documents (incorporation, charter, by-laws, etc.)
- Documents substantiating fixed asset additions
- Deeds
- Depreciation Schedules
- Financial Statements (Year End)
- General and Private Ledgers, Year End Trial Balances
- Insurance Records, Current Accident Reports, Claims, Policies
- Investment Trade Confirmations
- IRS Revenue Agents' Reports
- Journals
- Legal Records, Correspondence and Other Important Matters
- Minute Books of Directors and Stockholders
- Mortgages, Bills of Sale
- Property Appraisals by Outside Appraisers
- Property Records
- Retirement and Pension Records
- Tax Returns and Worksheets
- Trademark and Patent Registrations

Personal Documents To Keep For One Year

- Bank Statements
- Paycheck Stubs (reconcile with W-2)
- Canceled checks
- Monthly and quarterly mutual fund and retirement contribution statements (reconcile with year-end statement)

Personal Documents To Keep For Three Years

- Credit Card Statements
- Medical Bills (in case of insurance disputes)
- Utility Records
- Expired Insurance Policies

Personal Documents To Keep For Six Years

- Supporting Documents For Tax Returns
- Accident Reports and Claims
- Medical Bills (if tax-related)
- Property Records / Improvement and Renovation Receipts (keep up to six years after property is transferred or sold)
- Sales Receipts
- Wage Garnishments (keep for six years after the event has ended)
- Other Tax-Related Bills
- Bankruptcy Paperwork (keep for six years after the event has ended)

Personal Records To Keep Forever

- CPA Audit Reports
- Legal Records
- Important Correspondence
- Income Tax Returns (including Forms W-2's, 1099's, mortgage and charitable statements
- Income Tax Payment Checks
- Investment Trade Confirmations
- Retirement and Pension Records

Special Circumstances

- Car Records (keep until two years after the car is sold)
- Credit Card Receipts (keep with your credit card statement)
- Insurance Policies (keep for the life of the policy)
- Mortgages / Deeds / Leases (keep 6 years beyond the agreement)
- Pay Stubs (keep until reconciled with your W-2)
- Property Records / improvement receipts (keep until two years after property sold)
- Sales Receipts (keep for life of the warranty)
- Stock and Bond Records (keep for 6 years beyond selling)
- Warranties and Instructions (keep for the life of the product)
- Other Bills (keep until payment is verified on the next bill unless used for business purposes)
- Depreciation Schedules and Other Capital Asset Records (keep for 3 years after the tax life of the asset or last year depreciated on income tax return)

Many of these items can be scanned and saved to your hard drives or in the cloud. Be sure to look for our future publication on how to be organized in the electronic arena.

Mamie Brinkley

www.ustaxservices.com

info@ustaxservices.com

Author's Statement

Mamie Brinkley

Mamie Brinkley was raised and educated in the south region of the United States of America. She is a Licensed Public Accountant and Licensed Enrolled Agent. Over the years she has implemented many bookkeeping and accounting systems to assist her clients' in managing and reporting their financial matters. She has worked in banking and financial industries, Corporate America, governmental and nonprofit agencies. She has a high level of integrity, due-diligence and accuracy in performing her task as an accountant and tax professional.

Mamie is on the **precipice** *of sharing with the public many ideas and knowledge she has mastered over the years in this written publication.*

She has dealt with many unique people and situations. She has learned to seek out, research and use her experiences and knowledge as a guide to her significant future.

She is an advocate of understanding one's past in order to establish good business principles. Performing a historical exercise will greatly benefit your decisions and business success.

Rely on your instincts: they are inherited.

Rule for Success

Remember...there's a place for you on this earth. You are somebody, somebody different than any other somebody. With God's help, you can make of your life whatever you are determined to make of it. *"Arthur Unknown"*

A Note From the Author

"And a Voice
Shall
Rise From the
South…"

Mamie Brinkley

Notes

Notes

Notes

Notes

Notes

For additional copies of

S.Y.N.C -- Self-Employment, Your New Career

ORDER FORM

NAME: _____

ADDRESS: _____

CITY: _____ STATE: ___ ZIP CODE: _____

PHONE: (H) _____ (W) _____

E-MAIL ADDRESS: _____

Qty.	Product Description	Unit Cost	Total $
	(Please allow 2 - 3 weeks for delivery.)		
1	**Book:**		41.00

Total Order	$
Shipping & Handling	**Free Shipping**
Tennessee Sales Taxes: 9.75%	**4.00**
Grand Total	**$45.00**

METHOD OF PAYMENT ☐ CASH ☐ CHECK ☐ MONEYORDER

MAKE CHECK PAYABLE TO: Mamie Brinkley

Address: P. O. Box 40444, Nashville, Tennessee 37204-0444

Credit Card ☐VISA ☐MasterCard

Number: _____ Exp. _____

Signature_____ CVC: _____

E-mail: mab@syncthebook.com

Web site: http://www.syncthebook.com

Phone: 615.333.3330   Land Line Fax: 615.333.3332

Thank you for this journey…

Mamie Brinkley

S.Y.N.C.

www.ingramcontent.com/pod-product-compliance
Lightning Source LLC
Chambersburg PA
CBHW061315220326
41599CB00026B/4883